WHY BELIEVE?

Why Believe?

*Reason and Mystery
as Pointers to God*

C. Stephen Evans

William B. Eerdmans Publishing Company
Grand Rapids, Michigan / Cambridge, U.K.

Previously published in 1986 as
The Quest for Faith: Reason and Mystery as Pointers to God
by InterVarsity Press, Downers Grove, Illinois, and
Inter-Varsity Press, Leicester, England

This revised edition © 1996 by Wm. B. Eerdmans Publishing Co.
2140 Oak Industrial Drive N.E., Grand Rapids, Michigan 49505 /
P.O. Box 163, Cambridge CB3 9PU U.K.

Printed in the United States of America

16 15 14   11 10 9 8 7

Library of Congress Cataloging-in-Publication Data

Evans, C. Stephen.
    Why believe? : reason and mystery as pointers to God / C. Stephen
Evans. — Rev. ed.
        P.   cm.
    Rev. ed. of: Quest for faith. c1986.
    Includes bibliographical references and index.
    ISBN 978-0-8028-0127-2 (pbk. : alk. paper)
        1. Apologetics. 2. Faith and reason — Christianity. 3. Mystery.
I. Evans, C. Stephen. Quest for faith. II. Title.
BT1102.E44   1996
239—dc20   96-26078
                        CIP

www.eerdmans.com

To the Mitchells:
David, Dee, and Mark

Contents

Preface

LET'S CALL HIM Andrew. It was my first class as an independent instructor. I was inexperienced but enthusiastic as I set about initiating twenty-two students into the complexities of contemporary European philosophy. Andrew was my most appealing student. He was bright, outgoing, and friendly. We had long talks in and outside class.

As we got to know each other, Andrew became interested in my Christian faith. He found it appealing, but incredible. "I would think having that kind of faith would make life very satisfying," he said one afternoon. "I wish I could believe what you believe. But I just can't."

I tried my best to help Andrew see Christian faith as a live option, but I was, to my knowledge, unsuccessful. After spring vacation I received a brief note from the dean of students, requesting a meeting. There I was informed that Andrew had taken his own life.

Talking to Andrew's parents was one of the most difficult things I had ever done. They had no answers and neither did I. I didn't know why such a talented, seemingly happy young person would have committed suicide, and I still don't. His reasons may have had nothing to do with faith or his lack of it.

Still, something deep inside made me feel that somehow I had failed Andrew. I remembered the wistful tone in Andrew's voice as he expressed his envy of my faith. I learned, too, that Andrew's body had been discovered with several occult religious books spread open around him. Here was a young man who had been seeking for something I had. If I had been successful in communicating my faith to Andrew, I felt, things might have been different.

Besides frustration with my own personal failure, I felt angry at something difficult to define. I was angry at my culture, at the forms of thought that had surrounded Andrew and made it almost impossible for him seriously to consider Christianity — even though he so needed religious meaning that he was willing to look at religious ideas that were rather bizarre, with little intellectual credibility.

Someday I knew I would want to write a book for Andrew, and others like him I have met along the way. I'm sure there are many others in the same situation that I will never meet personally. As I explain in the first chapter, I am under no illusion that religious faith is usually or even ever the result of intellectual argument alone. The roots of faith lie much deeper. Still, the sense that Christian faith is simply unacceptable to a person with an intellect who cares about truth can be a powerful barrier to faith. This book is an attempt to remove that barrier. It will not do so for everyone, but I believe it may be helpful for those who are truly concerned about what life means and are willing to examine or reexamine deeply held assumptions and attitudes. If there is only one such person, I will feel that writing this book was worthwhile, for that one person may be an Andrew. Such a person I will call, following Kierkegaard, "that individual, whom with joy and gratitude I call my reader."

CHAPTER ONE

Thinking about Faith

The inescapable presence of doubt is a constant reminder of our responsibility to truth in a twilight world of truth and half-truth.

Os Guinness, In Two Minds

He found his doubts and gather'd strength
    He would not make his judgment blind,
    He faced the spectres of the mind
And laid them; thus he came at length
To find a stronger faith his own.

Tennyson, In Memoriam

JIM WATCHED Holly stride toward him. He liked Holly's walk; like everything about her it was cheerful, full of life and energy. It was good to see her again. He had met some attractive women at school this fall, but none of them kindled the special spark he felt for Holly. It was funny how he had taken her for granted in high school. How much more special she seemed now that they had spent a few months apart!

Holly hugged him. "Jim, it's great to see you; you're looking wonderful."

1

"Well, you look pretty good yourself, if these bleary eyes are any kind of judge. I sure had a lot of late-night crams during finals week."

"Now, Jim, you didn't study *that* hard at school. I know you better than that. Tell the truth. Your eyes are really tired from all those late-night parties."

Jim laughed. "And I suppose they don't have any parties at Ivy League schools?"

The small talk continued as they walked through the park. It was friendly, but Jim felt that there was something on Holly's mind, something she didn't quite know how to bring up. There was a long silence.

"Jim," Holly said at last. "You know in my last letter I said there was something important I wanted to talk with you about."

"Well, sure, Holly. You know I'd be glad to talk about anything on your mind."

"Jim, it's kind of hard for me to talk about this for several reasons. First, I don't really know where our relationship is, how serious you are about me, I guess, so I don't know if what I want to talk about is appropriate."

Jim felt both happy and embarrassed — happy because it was clear that Holly was still serious about him, embarrassed that he hadn't been more forthright with her about his feelings. He had put her into an awkward position.

"I guess I'm at fault there, Holly. I really do care for you, and I should have told you that plainly a long time ago. I don't think I'm ready for any permanent commitments right now, but I have to admit, when I think about the future, I sure think a lot about you."

Holly squeezed his hand and they walked along silently. Finally, Holly began to speak again, still a little hesitant.

"What I want to say, well, you know, when two people are serious about each other, then it's important that they share basic values, don't you think?"

"Why sure, of course."

"That's why we need to talk about Christianity, Jim. You see, last . . ."

"Oh, is *that* all you're worried about," Jim broke in with a relieved smile. "Holly, you don't have to worry about that any-more. I won't pressure you to go to church or anything. In fact, you'll be really surprised to find out how much I've changed in that whole area."

"Jim, you really should have let me finish," Holly said quietly, "but I'm certainly interested in hearing about the changes in your life."

"Well, Holly, you know in high school all of us thought your ideas on religion were a little different, to say the least. I couldn't understand why you wouldn't ever come to church with me, even to make my folks happy, or go to any of the youth group activities. I knew your father was an atheist, but I couldn't understand why you had to make such a big point of putting religion down."

"It's true, Jim. I was pretty hostile to your faith. I guess I saw it as a kind of psychological weakness, and I hated the hypocrisy of kids who felt the same way as I did, but went through the motions to please their parents."

"Well, maybe I was something of a hypocrite, Holly."

"Oh, I didn't mean you, Jim. I always felt you were sincere."

"Well, it doesn't matter, really, because I see now that you were right about a lot of things. In high school I was just too influenced by my parents, but I'll admit that I enjoyed the status of being leader of the youth group. But college has given me new perspective on some things."

"How so, Jim?"

"Basically I see now that religion is a prescientific way of thinking. And it's not innocuous, either. It may have been a good thing in the past, but today religion is one of the great forces holding back social progress."

Jim was echoing the words of his sociology professor, but the words didn't sound quite the same now as they had in the lecture hall. He continued quickly. "Oh, it's terribly complicated, of course; a lot more needs to be said. But still I think you were right all along."

"Well, Jim, I guess I have to tell you straight out. I don't think I was right all along. I've become a Christian."

Jim couldn't believe what he had heard. He felt stunned — annoyed too. Was this Holly talking to him, Holly who constantly had poked fun at him, calling him "Reverend" and tempting him to skip church on Sunday mornings and go with her to the beach? His reunion with Holly certainly wasn't going as he had expected.

"Come on, now. Are you trying to tell me that *you* have gotten religious?"

"That's not how I would describe it, Jim, but I suppose some people would."

"What do they teach in those Ivy League schools, Holly? I thought college was a place for stretching your mind." Jim regretted the remark as soon as he said it, but his irritation had gotten the better of him.

Holly was silent. Then she turned and looked Jim right in the eyes. "It's true that college is a time for questioning, Jim, and I can see that you've questioned a lot of things you just took for granted before. Me, I never took those things for granted. But I have thought about them and questioned what I used to believe. When I got to school I found my roommate was a Christian, of all things. We talked about faith a lot, and I saw something different in her. I really have made a commitment to Jesus Christ. I know it sounds funny coming from me, but I actually do believe he is the Son of God, and I want to follow him as best I can. I can't imagine life without him now, and anyone thinking about sharing in my life should know that."

Jim felt a little foolish. "Uh, Holly, I'm sorry I sounded so condescending. Of course you've got a right to your own ideas, and I respect your beliefs. We'll talk more about this later. I'll try to see you tomorrow."

Holly squeezed his hand again and Jim was off. The irritation had left him. Now he just felt confused.

Believing in the Contemporary World

The story of Jim and Holly reflects the problem of growing up in today's pluralistic world. In such a culture religious faith (or the lack thereof) cannot be taken for granted. The next person you meet won't necessarily think like you do.

Let's consider Jim's situation first. Jim was raised in a religious home and had a faith of a sort himself. Then, in a surprisingly short time at the university, he lost it. The causes for this may, of course, not be primarily intellectual. Nevertheless, at the university Jim was presented with a variety of distinctly contemporary problems that loom as barriers to faith for many people, older as well as younger.

One set of problems involves science and religion. Many people who rightly see that to be a Christian is to be committed to the truthfulness of the Bible are troubled by the creation account in the early chapters of Genesis. The Bible seems to them to teach that the earth was created quite recently, in a fairly short period of time, and that God created human beings in a special act. All this conflicts — or seems to — with the widespread view that the earth is tremendously old and that all of life, including human life, evolved by natural processes from inanimate matter.

The whole idea of miracles is also bothersome. A miracle seems to break or interrupt the natural order. To those who have a scientific mind-set, such interruptions may be difficult to accept. Water is turned to wine, a man walks on water, and people are raised from the dead — these stories are not easy for a modern mind to affirm.

The social sciences pose other obstacles to religious faith. Psychologists inform us that religion is a "crutch." People believe in God because they need to believe that the universe is not as unfriendly and impersonal as it appears. Furthermore, what people need to believe, or badly want to believe, they are usually able to believe. Human beings are not nearly so rational as they like to think.

Sociologists and anthropologists also debunk religion. They see it as a powerful tool that helps make individuals willing to sacrifice for the good of the society. The particular religion people hold and the manner they hold it are largely matters of social conditioning.

Social reformers and critics often weigh in at this point with claims that religious beliefs, especially Christian ones, are a barrier to social progress. The checkered historical past of Christendom, including Crusades, anti-Semitism, the destruction of Native American peoples, and slavery, is brought forward as proof of the socially reactionary character of religion. In the current situation some radical feminists hammer traditional religious belief as a main source of sexism and oppression of women.

Philosophers pose problems too, foremost among them the problem of suffering. Why, if God is so good and so powerful, does he allow so much evil and misery to go on in the world?[1]

All these ideas and more confront people like Jim today. To these barriers to faith we must add the fact that religion seems to lack positive rational support. It is not just that a lot of us have reasons for not believing, but that few of us have strong reasons for believing. It's not too surprising then that people like Jim, when they are separated from an environment in which religious faith functions as a kind of social necessity, find that faith is no longer a live option. Faith seems to such people to be something that exists largely among the uneducated. Educated people who still believe do so because of psychological hang-ups.

Yet there are also the Hollys, intelligent people who commit themselves to the cause of Jesus Christ in a serious way. Many come from religious homes. Some, like Holly, have no religious background. The question is, does Holly's decision make sense? Can an educated person who cares about truth honestly opt for Christian faith today? My purpose in this book is to show that both of these questions can be answered with a solid yes. I want to show Jim, and others like him, why Holly's decision is right, not just for her, but for any serious-minded person who cares about truth.

---

1. Here and throughout the book I refer to God by using male pronouns. Several of the great monotheistic religions, including Christianity, Judaism, and Islam, have traditionally referred to God in this manner, and many believers hold that this language is "authorized" by God's own self-revelation. However, theologians have always recognized that this does not imply that God is actually male. Rather, all these monotheistic faiths have held that God is spirit and has no biological sexual identity. Recently, some feminist theologians have criticized this traditional language. I discuss the question of whether Christian faith is sexist in Chapter Eleven. In using this traditional language I certainly do not mean to imply that God is literally male.

Why Not Suspend Judgment?

First, however, a major barrier must be faced: skepticism. Many people have given up trying to discover truth in this area. Isn't agnosticism more modest and reasonable? That is, shouldn't we suspend judgment because no one really knows the answers in the area of religion?

After all, a bewildering variety of faiths compete for our attention today. Besides all the different forms of Christianity and Judaism, resurgent non-Christian religions, such as Islam, Hinduism, and Buddhism, now confront us. Even pre-Christian pagan ways of thinking have been revived, and groups such as the Unification Church (Moonies) and the Hare Krishnas haunt airports and the corridors of our campuses. As the world shrinks and becomes more interdependent, the number of religious options has grown drastically. Small wonder we find agnosticism increasingly attractive. How can we sort through all these options?

Agnosticism: Modest and Hostile

Two kinds of agnosticism are possible in the area of religious belief. First, there is what I shall call the *modest agnostic*. Modest agnostics simply do not know what to think about religion. They are honestly perplexed. They don't deny that there is truth in this area, nor do they rule out the possibility that others may know about this truth. They simply know that they do not know it, at least not yet. Modest agnosticism of this type is frequently a reasonable position to hold. It enables people to arrive at convictions that will be genuinely their own. I hope that this book will be of help to modest agnostics who are thoughtfully considering Christianity.

The people I call *hostile agnostics* are very different. They don't just say that *they* do not know the truth about religion. Rather, they claim that no one does, and therefore everyone ought to give up their religious convictions. They are *religious skeptics*.

The attractions of religious skepticism are more apparent than real. To claim that I know that no one else knows anything about a particular area of knowledge is to claim a certain superiority over those who claim to know. This is not merely the superiority a modest agnostic may have, the advantage of a Socrates who is wiser than his contemporaries by recognizing his own limitations. It is the alleged superiority of a person who claims to be able to establish the powers and limits of the human mind. The hostile agnostic may not know the truth about religious matters, but such a person claims an almost godlike knowledge of the human condition.

Besides the presumption inherent in the hostile agnostic position, there is one further difficulty: Can we live as agnostics? What a hostile agnostic invariably forgets is that religious beliefs are not merely intellectual *theories*, about which we can easily suspend judgment. *Religious convictions concern life and how life should be lived.* And since we cannot suspend judgment about life itself, in the end we cannot be neutral about religious faith.

An example may make this clearer. Many religions teach that life after death is a reality and that our actions in this life may have an impact on our destiny after death. Imagine a religion that teaches (as some have) that to have a happy afterlife it is absolutely necessary to refrain from sexual intercourse in this life. Could a person suspend judgment about this? In a practical sense the answer is no. We may of course be somewhat unsure if this teaching is true. We might decide to abstain from intercourse on the chance the doctrine is true, or we might decide to ignore the doctrine because we think it unlikely to be true. But whether we refrain from sex or engage in sex, in a practical sense we are not being neutral. *Practically,* a person is either a believer or an unbeliever.

It is a failure to appreciate this practical dimension of faith that causes many self-professed agnostics to be oblivious to their own "faith." Classic examples of this are the signers of the *Humanist Manifestos I* and *II.* The authors of these declarations tell us plainly that humanity must be guided by reason, which they see as an instrument distinct from and superior to "faith and passion." Yet it is almost impossible to read these manifestos without being struck by how much they express the *faith* of the authors: faith in reason itself as our best guide; faith in "the scientific method" as the ultimate form of reason; faith "that mankind has the potential intelligence, good will, and cooperative skill" to realize the humanist program; faith that individual persons have a "preciousness and dignity."

These latter faiths are held despite the humanist conviction (equally a matter of faith) that nature is all there is ("any new discoveries . . . will but enlarge our knowledge of the natural") and that people are merely a product of impersonal evolution. For the humanist "the total personality is a function of the biological organism," functioning as it does "in social and cultural context."[2] They believe that despite their origin from an essentially meaningless universe, people have intrinsic worth and dignity, and possess almost boundless ability to improve themselves and their world. It is not as easy to avoid faith as the humanists think.

Marxists provide another interesting example of a group that supposedly rejects faith and opts for reason. Old-fashioned communists, now almost extinct, looked down on faith as a product of a decaying society. Yet who exhibited more faith than such old-time Marxists, who believed that a "workers' state" that owned the instruments of production would eventually transform human nature to such a degree that the state itself would no longer be needed but would "wither away." The failure of such dreams not only shows powerfully that the Marxist creed was chock-full of faith, but also reveals how weak the foundations of this faith in "scientific socialism" really were all along.

These examples and others suggest that having faith is a part of human nature. Each of us has a faith-dimension. None of us can avoid faith in something or someone. We must believe in something or someone because we must have something or someone to live for. If this is right, the hostile agnostic's advice to suspend judgment cannot really be followed. It is not a matter of whether to have faith, but of where faith is to be exercised.

Of course this does not mean that all beliefs are reasonable, or that people should not reflect on their deepest beliefs. As we shall see, the common stereotype of faith as "believing without

2. *Humanist Manifestos I and II,* ed. Paul Kurtz (Buffalo: Prometheus Books, 1973), 16-18, 23, 161.

any good reasons" rests on a naive understanding of both faith and reason.

My conclusion at this point is simply that we should never adopt a skeptical view at the beginning of religious inquiry. Taking such a position at the outset appears to be either lazy or cowardly. Given the modern religious situation, it may be difficult for us to discover the truth. But the difficulty, if real, should inspire us to further efforts if we really want the truth.

Perhaps we may finally be driven to conclude that we "just don't know" and end with modest skepticism. But such a conclusion should be a result of an honest search, not an excuse for not seeking. And a modest confession of personal ignorance of that sort is far removed from the immodest, dogmatic conclusion of hostile agnostics, who claim not only that *they* don't know the truth, but that no one else does either. To know *this,* a skeptic would need to know far more than most of us think is possible for a finite human being.

Giving Up on Truth

Another type of skepticism is probably even more prevalent in today's world than hostile agnosticism. The hostile agnostic may still believe in objective truth: either God exists or God does not exist; the agnostic just does not think it is possible for us to know such truth. Many would doubt this assumption of objective truth today.

Many people today exhibit an attitude that I first saw exhibited by Jane Fonda on a late-night talk show when I was in graduate school in the early seventies. (Yes, they had talk shows in those days, though they were a bit different in character from some of the current crop.) The actress was paired for some reason with the Archbishop of Canterbury and the subject turned to Christian belief. The Archbishop had just said something about the importance of Jesus for the contemporary world, to which Fonda, who was then in a radical phase, responded with incredulity. The venerable clergyman then said, with typical British understatement and an impeccable Oxford accent, "Well, he is the Son of God, you know." Fonda's response was one I have since heard from many students: "Well, perhaps he is to you, but not to me." The Archbishop replied quite simply, "Either he is or he isn't."

Now perhaps Fonda was only making a comment about the difference between her belief and the Archbishop's: "You believe Jesus is God, but I don't." If so, then she and the Archbishop could still agree there is an objective fact of the matter, but disagree about what that fact is. However, many people today make comments similar to Fonda's and intend to make a comment about truth itself. They seem to think that what a person believes is somehow *true for that person;* truth is not really objective at all.

Such a view of truth sometimes lies behind what I jokingly like to call "first-amendment relativism." Occasionally, when a person takes a strong stand on some moral and religious issue, and defends that view as true, others will respond, "You have no right to impose your belief on others. Everyone has a right to his or her own beliefs." Putting forward a conviction as objectively true, as a position that everyone should hold, is seen as infringing on other people's freedom.

I am of course a strong defender of freedom of thought, as well as of free speech. I would be among the first to protest any attempt to coerce the beliefs of anyone. Any attempt to produce belief or its semblance by threats or psychological manipulation is ethically repugnant. However, freedom of thought and belief can be recognized as precious without abandoning the quest for objective truth. In fact, it is just because truth is precious — and no finite human being has a monopoly on truth — that freedom of thought and belief must be protected. No state or church or educational establishment should try to coerce my beliefs, not because whatever I believe is true for me, but because my life is the one at stake if I fail to discover what is really true.

I cannot produce a proof that there is objective truth, but I can testify that this is the only kind of truth worth having. Like the Archbishop, I believe that Jesus is the Son of God, the one who died and now lives as the answer to human guilt and death. Perhaps some friend will see my belief as deluded, but yet think that it is kinder not to enlighten me. After all, maybe my belief is one that "works" psychologically for me, and I would be less happy without it. If I had a friend who did look at me in this manner, I could only see my friend's kindness as badly expressed.

We hear frequently that "Friends don't let friends drive drunk." I agree. But it seems to me that good friends also do not sit idly by and allow friends to achieve a false happiness that rests on an illusion. Hence a friend who tried to challenge my beliefs would be a true friend. If knowing Jesus is not the path to eternal life, I need to know this. And the Archbishop is ultimately right about the alternatives, even if he is wrong in his beliefs: "Either he is or he isn't."

I don't mean to suggest that I don't care about happiness; all of us who are honest will admit that we do care. However, I am convinced that true happiness is founded on truth; anyone who asks me to choose happiness over truth is offering me a false happiness.

In any case, even if my beliefs offer happiness (and I can testify that religious faith can sometimes bring unhappiness of a kind as well), they do so only if I am convinced they are objectively true. I may be comforted when I face death if I believe that Jesus *really* offers eternal life to me; it will be scant comfort to know that such a belief is not objectively true but merely psychologically comforting. It is hardly comforting simply to know that such a belief is comforting. If I don't really think that it is true that Jesus offers to me eternal life, then I don't really have the belief and can't be comforted by it. In the end, without faith in objective truth, religious faith does not "work" psychologically. Hence I cannot, without "bad faith" or self-deception, give up the quest for genuine truth.

Is Faith without Reasons Appropriate?

Even if we believe in objective truth, we may question the value of critical thinking about faith. Perhaps the whole idea of a rational inquiry into religious truth is misguided. Maybe people just can't be rational in this area. Faith of some kind — Christian, humanist, Marxist, or whatever — is inevitable and necessary. But in reality a person's faith is largely shaped by nonrational factors. We need only ask, who were his parents? What social or economic group did she come from? What did her peers think? and so on. To these sociological factors we could add psychological factors such as anxiety and guilt, and a person's need for security and autonomy.

I think we must concede that there is a great deal of truth in this line of thought, however unsettling this may be to human pride and our rational pretensions. Much of what any of us believes is the result, at least in part, of nonrational factors. This is no doubt easier to see in other people than in oneself, but it is still true.

Of course, this is not just true of Christians and Hindus, but equally true of humanists and Marxists. If it is true that the children of Christians are more likely to be Christians, it is equally true that the children of atheists are more likely to be atheists. If it is true that some people believe in God because they want to believe in a heavenly father, it is equally true that some people do not believe in God because they want to feel that they are masters of their own destiny, answerable to no one.

The fact that we are not completely rational in the adoption of our faith is not necessarily bad. Certainly it is not reasonable to claim that all of a person's beliefs should be the product of some explicitly conscious, logical process. Many of those human beliefs that might be termed "basic" or "foundational" seem to be beliefs that can't be traced back to any such process. And it would seem that there must be some beliefs of this character. Even though most of our beliefs are based on other beliefs, and those other beliefs may be based on still others, this chain of reasons cannot be infinitely long. Some of our beliefs must either have no basis at all or else be grounded in something different than other beliefs.

Think, for example, of the belief we all have that our fellow human beings are conscious beings like ourselves, not merely robots who behave as if they were conscious. Perhaps this belief can be given a rigorous philosophical proof, perhaps not. Philosophers disagree about such things. It is certain, however, that the vast majority of us don't hold this belief on the basis of any such proof. We have no more certain beliefs from which this belief can be derived. We just experience other people and *find ourselves believing* they have conscious minds. We find this belief irresistible and would regard someone who did not share it as very strange. Our inability to justify the belief to a philosophical skeptic does not bother us at all.

But could it ever be proper to hold a *religious* belief in such a simple, unreflective manner? Clearly religious beliefs *are* sometimes held in this manner. Some people find it impossible to believe in God; others find it impossible not to believe in God. Neither may be able to cite any rational proof for their position, or indeed, to give any reasons at all. They just find it totally obvious that there is (or isn't) a God. Are such people necessarily wrong-headed?

I do not think they are. Consider the following possibility. Suppose there is a God, and that it is very important for humans to know him and to relate to him in the proper manner. In such a situation God would surely make it possible for humans to get to know him in some way or other. One of the ways he might use would be to provide rational evidence from which people could logically infer his existence. But is it reasonable to think that this would be the *only* way God would make his existence known?

People differ greatly in their intelligence, reasoning ability, education, and so on. If the knowledge of God could be obtained *only* through a process of logical reasoning, then more intelligent people would have an advantage over less intelligent people in coming to know God. But this seems unfair; nor is it consistent with what most religions have maintained about the knowledge of God: intellectual ability doesn't necessarily lead to a better knowledge of God. Much more important are moral qualities like love, courage, and honesty. It seems reasonable then to think that God might use some methods besides reason to make his presence known (though of course he might use reason too).

A rationalist might claim that God could perhaps overcome this unfairness problem by making the intellectual evidence so strong and obvious that even the person of lowest intelligence could not fail to draw the right conclusion. Whether this is possible or not, I would question whether God, if he exists, would want to make his reality *that* obvious. For God presumably would want his creatures to serve him freely out of love, not simply out of fear of his power. If his reality were too obvious, then even the most selfish, mean-spirited person would believe in him and even (for selfish reasons) try to serve him. Even we humans believe that true love must be freely given, and we wouldn't value very highly someone who only "loved" us to get our money or avoid punishment. God, if he is real, must feel the same way. There is good reason to think, then, that God would give people "room" to reject him, because he only wants people to believe in him who are willing to believe in him.

It does not seem implausible then that God, if he exists, would make himself known to people by some method other than reason. Perhaps he might just implant in them a natural tendency to believe that he is real.[3] Perhaps he might provide those willing to know him with an experience or encounter with himself that would produce some kind of conviction.[4] The latter method seems particularly appropriate because it would lead not merely to a propositional knowledge about God, but to a personal knowledge of God himself.

I think it would be a mistake, therefore, to claim that a faith that is not based on reason is necessarily defective or inferior. Nonrational factors that lead to faith may well be part of the providence of God whereby people are brought into relation with him. (Perhaps an atheist could say that the nonrational factors that produce atheistic faith are part of the evolutionary process that is leading mankind to a better set of beliefs — *if* he or she has any reason to think evolution would lead to such a result!)

---

3. Theologian John Calvin, for example, held that human beings have a natural "sense of divinity," or *sensus divinitatis*, that would, if human beings were not sinful, make belief in God as natural as belief in other minds.

4. See Alvin Plantinga, "Reason and Belief in God," in *Faith and Rationality*, ed. Alvin Plantinga and Nicholas Wolterstorff (Notre Dame: University of Notre Dame Press, 1984), for a rigorous defense of the notion that belief in God may be reasonable even though it is not based on evidence. For Plantinga, religious belief may have a (nonpropositional) ground even though it is not based on reasons.

The Value of Thinking about Faith

Though faith does not have to be based on reasons, it would equally be a mistake to claim that rational thought about religion is completely impossible, or that it is without value if it is possible. Although the influence of nonrational factors is very great, it is possible to reduce their influence by becoming aware of them. And sometimes these discoveries, coupled with inquiry, can lead to change.

Holly, daughter of an outspoken atheist, began to doubt her atheism, did some reading and critical thinking, and was converted to Christianity. Jim, brought up in a religious home, discovered that his faith was largely a product of his upbringing. This awareness produced genuine doubts and led to atheism.

For someone who is troubled by doubt, rational reflection is inescapable. It simply is not possible to will all doubts away. To hide from problems is a sign that faith is in trouble. A belief is a belief that something is *true,* an accurate account of the way things really are. Evading intellectual problems sometimes is a confession that if we were to investigate things, we would find that what we believe is *not* the way things are. Such a belief is already deeply hedged with doubt. If we are truly honest we will want to face the issues, we will want to believe the truth. Insofar as our faith, religious or nonreligious, includes a commitment to truth and honesty, then that faith itself demands rational testing.

Rational inquiry of this sort will be focused very differently from much discussion of religion today. Many writers center their attention on whether religion is or is not socially useful, an aid or an impediment to progress. Or they try to find out whether religion is or is not psychologically beneficial, a contributor to neurosis or a buttress of mental health. Such questions are important and interesting, and the answers to some of them might bear on the question of truth. However, we must remember that the primary question about any religion is not whether it is useful but whether it is true. That is the question we must keep uppermost in our minds as we proceed to examine the reasonableness of Christian faith.

Our conclusions so far are very simple:

1. There are genuine intellectual difficulties that serve as barriers to religious faith for honest, concerned people today.
2. These difficulties should be faced squarely if a person is troubled by them and is able to think about them.
3. Faith of some kind, religious or secular, is unavoidable, since a person's faith is the basis of his or her life.
4. Though faith does not have to be based on reasons, honest, critical reflection on one's faith can have great value, both for religious believers and for those whose ultimate faith is in something other than God.

CHAPTER TWO

God in the Courtroom

A young man who wishes to remain a sound Atheist cannot be too careful of his reading. There are traps everywhere — "Bibles laid open, millions of surprises," as Herbert says, "fine nets and stratagems." God is, if I might say it, very unscrupulous.

C. S. Lewis, *Surprised by Joy*

As LOVERS OF OLD fifties television shows know, Perry Mason always won every case he tried, sometimes against impossible odds. Does God need a Perry Mason in today's world? Is he on trial? If so, who is the prosecutor and who is the defendant? What standards of proof and evidence are to be employed? And most important, who is the jury? Stay tuned as we consider one of the most interesting cases of all, the case of Christianity.

How Much Proof Do We Need?

Religious commitments have a direct bearing on how we live, and so it is probably not possible — or even desirable — for us to think about religion in a purely neutral, objective manner. Nonetheless we can still think deeply and honestly about our commitments. If my very life is at stake, I should be specially concerned that my convictions be true.

Most philosophical discussions of religion revolve around the notion of "proof." Many philosophers have put forward arguments as proofs of God's existence, and many others have offered refutations of these proofs. Although some of the issues that are debated in this context are relevant to our purposes, a good deal of this discussion is not particularly helpful to us.

First of all, these philosophical discussions are often complicated, technical, and hard to follow. All of this may be fine for professional philosophers, but it is of no help to ordinary people, even thoughtful, educated people. If God exists and has provided rational evidence as one way people can know about him, surely it would not require a Ph.D. in philosophy to understand this evidence.

Second, these philosophical discussions often concern only abstract, philosophical concepts of God. They talk about a God who doesn't make contact with the faiths we live by. We want to know if there is a God who can be worshiped and who cares about us. Very few care about Aristotle's Unmoved Mover. We want to consider the reasonableness of whole living faiths.

Finally, and most importantly, most philosophical discussions of the reasonableness of belief in God focus on one single argument. Critics have often taken advantage of this fact and employed a divide-and-conquer strategy. Thus a writer will first try to refute the "argument from design," then the "moral argument," and so on, concluding that, because none of the arguments is a successful proof, belief in God is unreasonable.

This procedure is objectionable in at least two ways. First, since the arguments are considered in isolation, no attention is given to the possibility that the arguments might have great force if taken collectively. One bit of evidence against a criminal may not be enough to convict him. The same may be said of a second or third bit, or any number of bits, when taken in isolation. If each bit does have some force, however, then all of the bits taken together may be more than enough to convict the accused and send him off to prison.

It is the fact that the cases for and against a religious life-view typically rest on the whole range of human experience that makes it so difficult to evaluate religious beliefs. Sometimes this is the reason that believers — as well as unbelievers — have difficulty in explaining the reasons for their beliefs. The problem is not that they have no reasons, but that they have too many reasons. It is hard briefly to summarize why it is that a particular perspective seems to be the one that makes the most sense of a person's life and all that a person knows.

The second objection to the typical philosophical critique of proofs of God's existence is that the standard of proof involved is usually fantastically high. What constitutes a "proof" anyway? This question is none too easy to answer. Must an argument be universally accepted to be a proof? Accepted by all sane people who consider it? Frequently something like this standard seems to be presupposed in these discussions, for key points in particular arguments are alleged to be defective merely because they are disputed by some antireligious skeptics. Such a concept of proof seems impossibly high.

It also seems unfair, since this is not the standard of proof we require for nonreligious areas. Consider a court of law, for example. In a criminal case, to convict a person a jury needs enough evidence to regard the accused as guilty "beyond reasonable doubt," not "beyond any *possible* doubt." Jurors are not required to overcome the objections an ingenious philosopher might devise to show that it is logically possible that the accused is innocent. To find a person guilty, the jury merely has to overcome those objections that a "reasonable person" would regard as significant.

In a criminal case, since a guilty verdict may send a citizen to prison, it is appropriate to demand proof in this strong everyday sense, which "excludes reasonable doubt." In other types of cases, even less "proof" may be needed. In a civil damage suit over an airplane crash, it is not necessary to prove beyond any reasonable doubt that the crash was due to the airline's negligence, but only that it seems highly likely or probable "in the judgment of a prudent person" that it was so. The task in this sort of case is to make a judgment that is in accordance with "the preponderance of the evidence." A "clear and convincing proof" in this context is defined in terms of "a high probability." This seems to me to be the kind of "reasonable case" we ought to strive for in religious matters as well. We ought to strive to make a judgment that is in accord with "the preponderance of evidence" and that seems highly probable or plausible.

Is Religion Guilty until Proven Innocent?

One might think that these legal analogies imply that where the stakes are greater, such as in a criminal trial that might send a person to prison, it is appropriate to demand greater evidence. This principle is in general correct. Since the stakes religion poses are great indeed, potentially including eternal happiness, this would imply that the highest standard of proof should be adopted.

It is true, I think, that since religious faith is so significant, we ought to seek all the evidence we can and consider that evidence with great care and seriousness. However, at this point our legal analogies begin to fail us, because of the notion of "burden of proof." In a criminal court proceeding, the accused person is assumed to be innocent until proved guilty. Hence the burden of proof clearly rests with the prosecution.

Many skeptics apparently presume religious belief to be not innocent, but guilty until proven otherwise.[1] They think that the "burden of proof" is on religious believers. Unless we can prove God's existence, we must refrain from believing.

Religion and the Loch Ness Monster

People who think like this imagine the religious situation to be something like the following: Suppose you are having an argument

1. Michael Scriven and Antony Flew both have defended the claim that there is a "presumption in favor of atheism." See Antony Flew, *The Presumption of Atheism* (London: Pemberton, 1976), 14-15; and Michael Scriven, *Primary Philosophy* (New York: McGraw-Hill, 1966), 102-3. This presumption is clearly rejected by philosophers such as Alvin Plantinga and Nicholas Wolterstorff in *Faith and Rationality*.

with someone over how many species of animals exist. Both of you agree that there are many species — cats, dogs, cows, and so on. You, however, believe in one species that your opponent does not believe in — say the species of monsters residing in the Loch Ness. Your opponent claims that the burden of proof is on you if you want to believe in such monsters. Without strong *positive* evidence you would do better to refrain from believing in the Loch Ness monster.

Perhaps in this situation the burden of proof would be on you to come up with evidence for your belief. Perhaps if that evidence is less than conclusive it would be wiser to suspend or withhold judgment. After all, we don't usually believe in monsters if we have no evidence of their reality. But belief in God is not at all comparable to belief in such a monster.

One important difference is that the Loch Ness monster is merely "one more thing." The two people who disagree about the monster agree about all the other animals. God, however, is not merely "one more thing." The person who believes in God and the person who does not believe in God do not merely disagree about God. *They disagree about the very character of the universe.* The believer is convinced that each and every thing exists because of God and God's creative activity. The unbeliever is convinced that natural objects exist "on their own," without any ultimate reason or purpose for being. In this situation there are no neutral "safe" facts all parties are agreed on, with one party believing some additional "risky facts." Rather, each side puts forward a certain set of facts and denies its opponent's alleged facts. There is risk on both sides.

A second important difference between the case of God and the case of the Loch Ness monster is the one we pointed out earlier — religious beliefs imply something fundamental about how life should be lived. Insofar as religious beliefs embody themselves in actions, suspending judgment is not possible. Even if it were possible to suspend judgment intellectually, it would by no means enable a person to avoid risk. It is clear that the faith of the religious believer and the faith of the atheist are equally risky. It is hard to see why any special burden of proof falls on the religious believer.

You Are the Jury

Rational inquiry into religious faith should not, therefore, be viewed as a case in which faith is assumed guilty until proven innocent. There are several important respects, however, in which such inquiry does resemble a legal case. One is simply that the judgment one makes will depend on the total evidence available. Trying to look for a single isolated argument on either side to serve as a "proof" is therefore a mistake. Rather, each side here will present a range of facts, drawn from many areas of human experience, to show that the "preponderance of evidence" is on its side. Meanwhile, each side will try to show that the facts that the other side puts forward do not really prove the other side's case or damage its own. Rather, each party in the dispute tries to show how those facts can be interpreted so as to support or at least fit one's own case.

It is clear, I think, that such a debate can never be settled in a mechanical fashion by simply adding up "points scored." To a large extent how a person evaluates the evidence will be a matter of proper interpretation and good judgment. But this is also true of legal cases. We are not yet to the stage (and hopefully never will be) where legal cases can be decided by computers. Jurors and judges make many decisions for which no formal rules can be given. If they are honest, reasonable people of good sense and judgment, they will make those decisions well. In the area of religious faith, each of us is our own juror. We should strive to make similarly wise judgments.

A Look Back and a Look Ahead

My principal conclusion in this chapter is simply that the case for or against religious faith is in several important ways analogous to the kinds of cases employed in legal trials. Let me try to list some of the most significant parallels:

1. Good evidence for religious faith will not be the absolute proof that some philosophers have looked for, but will be evidence that is sufficient to satisfy a reasonable person.

2. The case for religious faith will not be based on a single
   argument functioning as a proof, but on the total evidence
   available from every region of human experience.
3. Religious faith is not guilty until proven innocent. No
   special burden of proof rests on the religious believer, since
   opponents of religious belief are committed to worldviews
   that are equally risky.
4. The evidence for religious faith cannot be evaluated in a
   mechanical fashion, but must be sensitively interpreted by
   each of us, who must ultimately take responsibility for
   being our own juror.

In the remainder of this book I will attempt to show that a
reasonable "cumulative case" can be made for a particular kind
of religious faith: Christianity. Drawing on philosophy, personal
religious experience, and historical evidence, I will try to show that
we have very good reasons to think that the Christian faith is true.
What one might call the Christian view of things makes sense of
a very wide range of facts, which its rivals either cannot explain
or else cannot explain very well. On the other side, the facts that
those rivals put forward can be accounted for by Christianity.
Besides building a positive case for Christianity we will also look
in detail at the problems that may have been behind Jim's loss of
faith: Is Christianity consistent with science? Can a reasonable
person believe in miracles? Would a good God allow evil to occur?
If Christianity is true, why have so many professed Christians been
responsible for so many dreadful things?

One final word of caution may be in order. (This will be of
more interest to Christians than to others.) Many Christians insist
that in the final analysis people are moved to faith by the Spirit
of God, not by human argument. I think the positive part of this
assertion is correct, and I have already agreed that many people
are brought to faith by nonrational factors. Such a faith is by no
means necessarily defective or inferior. The Spirit of God may,
however, use intellectual argument as one means of drawing us to
faith. At the very least, a reasonable case for faith can remove
barriers to the work of God's Spirit. Moreover, Christian faith
demands honesty and a sincere commitment to truth. Even those

drawn to faith by nonrational factors may want, precisely because of their faith, to see whether that faith can stand up to the test of reflection. None of us, however, should think that an intellectual understanding of faith can be a substitute for faith itself.

CHAPTER THREE

God and Santa Claus

<hr />

"Why," he [the priest] asked, "don't you let me come to
see you?"

I [Meursault] explained that I didn't believe in God.

"Are you really so sure of that?"

I said I saw no point in troubling my head about the
matter; whether I believed or didn't was, to my mind, a
question of so little importance.

Meursault in Albert Camus, *The Stranger*

"YES, VIRGINIA, there is a Santa Claus." With these famous words
a little girl was reassured that a cherished childhood conviction
was true. The spirit of Christmas that the story about Santa embodies is a reality, and thus in a deep sense Virginia was not wrong
in believing in Old St. Nick.

Yet there surely is a sense in which Virginia was wrong about
some of her beliefs. She probably believed that Santa was a fat
man who lived at the North Pole making lots of toys and then, in
one fabulous evening, visited every house in the world. If this is
what Virginia thought, she was indeed wrong.

I still remember a conversation I had several years ago with
my daughter Lise, who was then five years old. "Dad, is there
really a Santa?" Lise asked. Wanting neither to puncture a

26

cherished belief nor to be untruthful, I tried to finesse the question with the old "Yes, Virginia" line. "Christmas is a time of giving and sharing, and the story about Santa is a fun way to express this."

Lise was not satisfied. The spirit of Christmas is all fine and dandy, but she wanted to know if there *really* was a man who comes down chimneys. If so, how does he pull off the trick?

On looking at the question of God, many would prefer the ambiguities of "Yes, Virginia." Whether God exists or not, they reason, surely we can all believe in the ideals he represents, the ideals we feel are worthy of reverence.

Occasionally, however, we sense that such an answer is not satisfying. Like Lise we want to know if God *really* exists. Is there really a Person who made the universe? Does he know about us and care about us? Are the ideals we reverence simply our own inventions, or are they grounded in a reality and a power higher than our own? Of course we sense that the question about God's reality is not quite like the question of Santa's factual reality. God is not to be thought of as a kindly old man residing on a cloud somewhere just beyond the reach of jet planes. We understand that to ask about God is not merely to ask about another finite object within the universe. Nevertheless, there remains in the question about God an objective factual dimension: When we pray, either there is someone who hears us or there is not.

Meursault in Camus's *The Stranger* claims to be uninterested in the question of God's reality. But Meursault is surely unusual here. Most people, including atheists and agnostics, have an interest in whether or not God is real. But whether people are interested in the question or not, they *should be*.

The question of God cannot be finally avoided, because it is a question about what kind of a universe we live in. This is a real question and it must have a real answer. We need to know the truth about God if we are to live our lives rightly.

The Question of God

The question of God is central for Christians because a central element in Christian belief is belief in God. No reasonable case for the truth of Christianity can avoid facing whether belief in God is reasonable. Of course many who are not Christians believe in God as well. The concept of God in Judaism is to a large degree identical with that accepted by Christians. Islam also includes a belief in a God similar to Christianity's in many important respects. So a belief in God by itself is by no means equivalent to Christian faith, nor would showing that it is reasonable to believe in God necessarily mean it is reasonable to be a Christian.

Still, if God does not exist, Christianity cannot be true. It is fundamental to Christian belief that God created the world, that he created human beings to enjoy fellowship with himself by living lovingly and justly, and that he has acted decisively in Jesus Christ to reconcile his rebellious creatures with himself. Obviously, if there is no God, God could have done none of these things. The reasonableness of belief in God is clearly of preeminent importance to Christians.

It is important, of course, to be clear about *which* concept of God we refer to. People use the term *God* in many ways today. Some use it in a "Yes, Virginia" way to designate worthy human ideals. Some use it to refer to an order and purposefulness that they sense in nature. And some theologians and philosophers use it to refer simply to "being itself."

When I use the term *God,* I mean by it what Christians have meant for centuries. God is a personal being, whose existence is distinct from nature, since he created nature.[1] He is perfectly just and perfectly loving, and he is unlimited in his power and knowledge. He cares about human beings and is capable of communicating with them and acting in special ways in the course of nature

---

1. To reiterate a point made in a note to Chapter One, in using these traditional male pronouns I of course do not mean to imply that God is literally male. (Traditional theologians of course did not mean to imply this either.) God has no body and no sexual identity.

and human history, both of which are continuously dependent on him and ultimately controlled by him.

This is by no means an exhaustive account; Christians believe many more things about God. Some of these other beliefs, such as the claim that God is not a simple unity but is three-in-one, will be discussed later. But this should be sufficient to make it clear that when I speak about God I am speaking about someone we can worship and pray to.

Clues to God's Reality

Why should a person believe in God? It is important to see that in asking this question we are not asking why people do believe in God. The actual psychological factors that lead people to believe are various indeed and complicated in the extreme. Many of these factors, as we saw in discussing the origin of "faith" in the first chapter, are doubtless nonrational. As we saw there, this is not necessarily a bad thing. Our concern is whether or not there are good reasons to believe in God, evidence that would be convincing to a person willing and able to weigh it properly.

What kind of evidence should we attempt to find? Certainly we want to find the best evidence we can, evidence that is clear and strong. There is good reason to think, however, that God might not provide just any kind of evidence. It may not be important to God to see only *that* humans get to know about him; he may equally be concerned with *how* they get to know him.

We noted in the first chapter that the traditional Christian view of God is that he wants his human creatures to serve him freely out of love, not simply out of fear of his power or out of selfish desire. Since God is all-powerful, it is hard to see how a person who was clearly aware of God's existence could avoid wanting to obey him, even if he hated God rather than loved him. It seems plausible then that God would not provide evidence of his reality that would be absolutely undeniable, the kind of evidence that would force even the most hardened cynic to believe whether he wished to or not. Rather God would give unbelievers the "space" to reject him if they wished to.

If this is right, then it is likely that if God has provided evidence for his reality, he has provided evidence that will be *possible* for the determined unbeliever to discount or reinterpret. To see evidence as good evidence we must have the skill and sensitivity to properly "read" and interpret it. This ability to read and interpret the evidence properly is at least part of what is meant by the claim that God can be known only by faith. Faith is not believing without good reasons, as many think. It is, partly at least, a set of skills or abilities; it is the ability to see good reasons as good. Good evidence therefore will clearly point to God's reality, but it will not do so in a coercive fashion.

Of course this situation is not unique to religion. Evidence in legal cases must be interpreted, as must the evidence for historians, literary critics, and so on. Even the results of scientific experiments must be interpreted before they can be employed to support hypotheses. For this reason one can rightly say that something like faith is an ingredient in all forms of knowledge, for all human knowledge presupposes certain skills or abilities on the part of knowers. People acquire these abilities in the course of becoming part of the community of historians, or literary critics, or whatever community is involved. In a similar way, the community of faith tries to help new members gain the ability to see certain kinds of truth. So, when the religious believer views the evidence for God's existence as clues that point to his reality, even though they do not make it impossible for the unbeliever to refuse to believe, her stance is not unusual. Nor is it odd for her to claim that certain abilities, those summarized in the concept of faith, are necessary in order to see those clues.

What kinds of clues are there for the reality of God? Many Christians would say that the most fundamental and obvious clues are God's revelatory actions in human history. They believe that over a long period, God has actively made himself known to people. He called Abram and made him Abraham, the father of many nations. He revealed himself to Moses and gave the children of Israel the Ten Commandments. He performed mighty miracles through prophets such as Elijah and Elisha. He revealed himself decisively in the person of Jesus. All these and more are of course recounted in the Bible, viewed by Christians as a "special" revelation from God, written by humans through divine inspiration.

If God has revealed himself in this way to human beings, then this is impressive evidence of his reality. Christians who believe in God because they believe God has acted and spoken to them through Jesus in the Bible may be eminently reasonable. (We will discuss the whole idea of special revelation later on.) However, even if God has revealed himself in the way Christians believe, it is worthwhile to see if there is evidence for God's reality that is independent of what is accepted by Christians as special revelation.

The reason for this is that people today often find it difficult to believe that God has acted in history or that the Bible is a revelation from God. They find this hard because they are already convinced that God does not exist and, in fact, that the whole realm of the supernatural is a myth. For them, strong reasons for belief in God that are independent of one's acceptance of the Bible or Jesus as an authority are especially valuable. If there is a God, and we can know that he exists, then there is little basis for the dogmatic claim that God cannot reveal himself in human history. A mind more open to the possibility of a special revelation from God will be warranted. Even if a skeptic does not find the case for God's reality to be conclusive, at least dogmatic confidence in atheism may be weakened. If God's existence seems to be a genuine possibility, then we all ought to be alert to any additional evidence God might care to provide.

The actual clues God has provided for his reality, leaving aside the Christian claims that God has intervened in human history, center on three fundamental mysteries. We bump up against them time and time again: the mystery of the physical universe, the mystery of a moral order, and the mystery of human personhood. The next three chapters focus in turn on these three mysteries.

CHAPTER FOUR

The Mysterious Universe

Certain it is that a conviction, akin to religious feeling, of the rationality or intelligibility of the world lies behind all scientific work of a high order. . . . This firm belief, a belief bound up with deep feeling, in a superior mind that reveals itself in the world of experience, represents my conception of God. . . . Denominational traditions I can only consider historically and psychologically.

Albert Einstein, reply to a Japanese scholar

I cannot make my peace with the randomness doctrine: I cannot abide the notion of purposelessness and blind chance in nature. And yet I do not know what to put in its place for the quieting of my mind. It is absurd to say that a place like this place is absurd, when it contains, in front of our eyes, so many billions of different forms of life, each one in its way absolutely perfect, all linked together to form what would surely seem to an outsider a huge spherical organism. We talk — some of us anyway — about the absurdity of the human situation, but we do this because we do not know how we fit in, or what we are for.

Lewis Thomas, *On the Uncertainty of Science*

THE MYSTERY OF the universe is not a single mystery, but a cluster of mysteries. Several of the pervasive characteristics of the universe constitute mysteries in their own right. But beyond the special character of the universe there is the overriding mystery of the sheer existence of the universe.

Clue Number One: Cosmic Wonder

What is mysterious about the existence of the universe? Of course we do not always or even usually find the universe mysterious. Our normal attitude is simply to take it for granted. The universe is a fact. What more could we want?

But we do want more. For all of us at times, and for some more frequently than others, the universe is not something to be taken for granted, but something to be wondered about. We conceive many alternative universes, some very different from ours indeed. Why, out of all these possible universes, does ours exist? Or, to push our wonder one step deeper, why should any universe exist at all? Why shouldn't there just be nothing?

To someone in the grip of our everyday concerns, these questions may seem abstract and unnatural. But in certain experiences they become very natural and concrete indeed. I shall attempt to describe these experiences; perhaps readers will understand what I am talking about better than I do myself.

Like most people, I suppose, I am often struck by the thought that I might never have existed. "Where were you before your father was born?" asks a Zen master. This is a difficult thought to hold on to, perhaps even more difficult than imagining one's own death. Nevertheless, I can attach some sense to the idea.

I know my parents might never have met, or that they might not have had any children. At times I feel strongly that I might never have been. At certain points, however, I have been gripped by a further sensation. This strong feeling of "might-never-have-been" that I find attached to myself gets extended to my parents. They too might never have been. The same is true of course for their parents, and all my relatives and friends. At this point, if I can avoid a feeling of vertigo as my world seems to crumble, I feel quite strongly that this characteristic of might-never-have-been extends to the entire universe. Everything I perceive around me seems to be the sort of thing that in fact exists, but didn't have to. Everything seems to cry out, "Why? Why do I exist? There must be a reason for all of this."

This line of thought stems from "cosmic wonder." For different people it is engendered in different ways. For some it comes from contemplating the wonders of nature, gazing into a vast, starry sky or pondering a soft, dreamy sunset. For others, it comes at a birth or at the death of a friend or relative. But I am convinced that this experience is genuine and almost universal.

Skeptics may say that we are making way too much of an isolated experience, and possibly they are right. But it is also possible that such exceptional experiences reveal something that our everyday, superficial attitudes cover up.

For the believer, cosmic wonder is an important clue to God's reality. The characteristic of might-never-have-been that is discerned in the universe, including ourselves, is a true feature of the way things are. For all of these things might never have been. They were all freely created by God. One might say that the experience of cosmic wonder is an experience of the createdness of the natural order, a clue to the origin of natural objects, a calling card from the Creator. The strong sense that there must be a reason for these things is the natural response of a creature capable of experiencing creatureliness and wondering about it.

The characteristic of might-never-have-been that we have been discussing is traditionally called *contingency* by theologians and philosophers. The contingency of natural objects has been used by philosophers to develop what is termed the *cosmological argument* for God's existence. Indeed, precise arguments can be developed along these lines. It is important to see, however, that the argument we have developed is not understandable only by philosophers. It is rather a natural inference from a basic human experience — precisely the sort of clue we would expect to find if God is real and wants to provide us with evidence of his reality.

Clue Number Two: The Mystery of Purposive Order

Though the experience of cosmic wonder is impressive, by itself this clue to God's reality hardly constitutes an overwhelming case. This is why it is crucial to see this clue in the context of the other clues. It is the cumulative case that is significant.

Most people find the actual *character* of the universe even more mysterious and impressive than its bare existence. The existence of a universe in which we experience "might-never-have-been" is surprising and mysterious. But the universe is even more wondrous when we look at its actual nature. For our universe is incredibly intricate and orderly. From the smallest flower that blows to the grand show of the heavens, the universe shows itself to be marvelous. Could it not have been far more disorderly and chaotic? Could it not have been less beautiful and grand? But there it is — a marvel of magnificence.

This experience of "purposive order" is so powerful that even philosophers who are skeptical of the value of arguments for God's existence cannot help but acknowledge its force. David Hume, for example, the eighteenth-century Enlightenment thinker who was a renowned critic of all the standard philosophical proofs of God's existence, wrote that "a purpose, an intention, or design strikes everywhere the most careless, the most stupid thinker; and no man can be so hardened in absurd systems, as at all times to reject it."[1]

In a strange passage another Enlightenment philosopher, Immanuel Kant, who is often credited with having decisively refuted the argument from the order in nature to God's reality, nevertheless confesses that "by one glance at the wonders of nature and the majesty of the universe" reason is "at once aroused from the indecision of all melancholy reflection, as from a dream."[2]

Kant says that our sense of the mystery of the character of

1. David Hume, *Dialogues Concerning Natural Religion* (Indianapolis: Bobbs-Merrill, 1946), 214. Hume puts this statement in the mouth of Philo, the character in the dialogue who is the strongest critic of arguments to God from nature. Most scholars agree that Philo generally represents Hume's own views. Also see Philo's comments at 202.

2. Immanuel Kant, *Critique of Pure Reason,* trans. Norman Kemp Smith (New York: St. Martin's Press, 1965), 520.

the universe can be dimmed, at least temporarily, by philosophical speculation. Hume implies that at least for a time a person who is already firmly committed to an "absurd system" may lose this sense of wonder. No doubt the routine grind of daily living, the pressure to earn one's livelihood, the clatter of technology that insulates one from nature — all these can blunt our sense of the marvelous character of nature. But that by no means shows that our experience is not genuine and revelatory of something deep.

Does Evolution Dim Design?

Perhaps the greatest barrier to the experience of purposive order today is a misunderstanding of science. In the era before modern science, people who carefully examined the intricate organic systems of animals could not help but see these as evidence of design. The complexity and interrelatedness of the many parts of organic systems clearly seemed to point to an organized structure that was not a mere accident. Today some are inclined to think that this impression of purposive order is a mistake. After all, the whole business can be explained scientifically by evolution.

Since I am not a scientist, it is not my purpose here to evaluate the theory of evolution. Some Christians have of course attacked this theory, while many others accept it as the best scientific account we have about the origin and development of life. What I want to challenge is the notion that evolution, assuming the theory is scientifically true, provides us with a reason to discount the experience of purposive order.

At bottom our experience of order has two dimensions. First, we experience the world as possessing structure; and second, we experience that structure as in some way good, because it makes possible many beautiful and valuable things. If the theory of evolution is true, then the intricate structure that we perceive in nature is dependent on an even deeper level of order. The fundamental laws of nature itself have operated over a very long period so as to bring about this marvelous world.

Does the fact that science can explain the visible order by a still deeper, invisible order decrease the order or the value that depends on that order? It is hard to see why it should. The theory of evolution, then, even if it is true, should not lessen our wonder at nature's purposiveness. If evolution is true, then the visible order that is so manifest around us is shown to be dependent on a deeper, invisible order: the laws of nature and the fundamental properties of matter.

It is true that many popularizers of evolutionary theory see the theory as making God unnecessary. However, it seems to me that those who think this way either have ceased to wonder about the orderliness of the natural world or else do not think about the mysteriousness of the deeper fundamental natural order that makes the whole grand show possible. A God who accomplishes some of his purposes through an intricate and elegant set of orderly natural processes seems no less intelligent and powerful than a God who achieves all his goals by immediate fiats. In any case, despite the scientific popularizers who claim that science has made God unnecessary, many of the greatest scientists both in the past and today — people such as Isaac Newton and Albert Einstein — have been religious. Their deep understanding of the natural order increased rather than decreased their sense of awe in the face of nature.

A Deeper Clue

The experience of purposive order is simply our amazement that the world is as it is. It just strikes us very immediately that this kind of order is not simply an accident or the result of chance. The believer in God sees the order in nature as a clue that God has planted to witness to himself — a clue noted far back in human history. "The heavens are telling the glory of God," the Hebrew psalmist wrote (Ps. 19:1). And the apostle Paul claims that the invisible reality of God can be seen from the visible things God has made (Rom. 1:20).

Once more this seems to be just the sort of clue we would expect God to grant people if he is real. It is universally accessible and easy to grasp. Yet it is noncoercive. Those who wish to interpret away this clue can easily do so. They may even in time be able to dim their sense of this mystery altogether.

What is the clue a clue to? Here is where the experience of purposive order cuts deeper than the experience of cosmic wonder. The experience of cosmic wonder merely suggests there is a reason why all the things in the universe exist. Something or someone is behind it all, but that something or someone is very vague. The experience of purposive order suggests, however, that what is behind nature, the reason for the whole show, must be something like a mind, something with intelligence. For where things happen in an orderly way, where there is pattern or structure that brings about value, there mind is at work.

If we drive south from Tennessee down a highway and see on a hillside ahead a long string of rocks spelling out "Welcome to Georgia," we will never attribute this to chance.[3] It is of course *possible* that those rocks simply fell into that arrangement by chance, but it is exceedingly unlikely. If we do think it is chance, we certainly will not trust the information the sign seems to provide. Even if we were to observe the rocks falling into place by natural processes, we would, I think, be inclined to think that it was no accident and that those natural processes themselves were directed by intelligence.

The order and structure of signs pales in comparison to the order of the human brain. Yet the brain, like the sign, is accepted by us as a reliable source of information. If the brain cannot be explained by the process of nature, it clearly seems to be the creation of a mind. If it was produced by natural processes, as many modern scientists believe, then it looks as if those natural processes themselves are the result of mind. Either way, ultimately there is Mind behind the universe.

3. This kind of example is taken from Richard Taylor, *Metaphysics,* 3rd ed. (Englewood Cliffs, NJ: Prentice-Hall, 1983), 99-102.

CHAPTER FIVE

The Mystery of the Moral Order

Two things fill the mind with ever new and increasing admiration and awe, the oftener and more steadily we reflect on them: the starry heavens above me and the moral law within me.

Immanuel Kant, *Critique of Practical Reason*

Dostoievsky said, "If God didn't exist, everything would be possible." That is the very starting point of existentialism. Indeed, everything is permissible if God does not exist, and as a result man is forlorn, because neither within him nor without does he find anything to cling to.

Jean Paul Sartre, *Existentialism*

THE EXPERIENCE OF cosmic wonder is a clue that there is something or someone behind nature. The experience of purposive order suggests that something is more like a someone, in that it seems to possess intelligence. Beyond that these two experiences cannot take us very far. We might reason that the Mind is very great and powerful because of the vastness of nature and the intricacy of its design. We might conclude that the Designer is a great artist

39

because of the beauty that is so evident in nature. But what is this Mind, if it exists, really like? What is its character? These two experiences help us little here.

This is why the third experience is crucial. This is the experience of moral order: the experience of good and evil, and the sense of "ought" that is so basic to the human condition.[1]

The Reality of Moral Law

The experience of "ought" is fundamental and pervasive. We feel it most keenly during periods of temptation, when we strongly desire to do something we feel just as strongly we shouldn't.

When he fills out his income tax, Jerry badly wants to forget the $500 he received for playing his trumpet at weddings last year, but he knows he ought to report the income. In a job interview Sue badly wants to leave out some important information about why she was dismissed from her last job, but she feels she ought to tell the truth. Jane is dying to tell Joe that delicious little rumor she heard about Henry, but she knows deep down that it would be wrong to pass on such gossip.

What do such experiences mean? Simply that there is a standard of behavior we are all aware of, one that we all know we ought to live up to. Some call this morality, others ethics; some just term it common human decency.

There are several surprising features of morality as we experience it. First, though this standard is clearly our standard (some have called it the "law of human nature"), it is a standard that we commonly violate. If we are honest with ourselves, we know there are many times when we have been less honest, less caring, less courageous than we should have been. If we are not perceptive enough or honest enough to see it in ourselves, we certainly see it in others.

1. The following argument closely parallels the argument C. S. Lewis developed from morality to God's existence. See C. S. Lewis, *Mere Christianity* (New York: Macmillan, 1952), chs. 1-5.

This standard, this "law" if you will, is therefore not simply a description about how people behave. It is a prescription about how people should behave, though one they are constantly violating. So morality is not simply a law of nature like the law of gravity. It doesn't describe how things in nature go on, but how human behavior ought to go on.

The second surprising feature is that though this law of morality or human decency is not simply a description of how things are, it seems no less real. Though we constantly excuse ourselves when we fall short of the standard, we sense that the existence of the standard doesn't depend on what we think and want. If John knows he has been nasty or cruel, he feels he has been bad. John probably doesn't like this truth very much. He probably can think of five wonderful reasons for his behavior, or explanations for it. We all do this. But the fact that we try so hard to excuse ourselves and even to deceive ourselves shows that we are aware that the standard exists. If we have done something we ought not to have done, then we have in fact done it, like it or not.

Again, this is much easier to see in others than in ourselves. It is patently obvious that children should not be sexually abused. It is obvious that all kinds of violent, cruel, and greedy acts that are done every day ought not to be done.

Now what are we to make of this surprising fact? It seems to indicate that in addition to the physical order that provokes the experience of purposive order, there is another kind of order in the universe: a moral order. It is right to be kind, generous, honest, courageous, and just. It is wrong to be selfish, cruel, deceptive, and cowardly. It is wrong to be abusive, unfriendly, and ungrateful. These are truths that human beings discover. We do not invent them; in their own way they are as objective as the laws of science or mathematics.

Doubts about the Moral Law: Cultural Relativism

Many people are inclined to doubt this, of course. At least they are inclined to doubt it when they are theorizing about morality.

The standard of morality is much harder to doubt when one is engaged in some activity, and is even harder to doubt when one is being mistreated by others.

People express various kinds of doubt about the objectivity of morality. One popular doubt is that morality is merely a product of culture. Every culture teaches its young that some approved actions are "right" and other disapproved actions are "wrong." The strength of this view is that it explains why different cultures differ in what is considered "right" or "wrong." But it is hard for this kind of "cultural relativist" to explain why there are also strong similarities between what is regarded as right and wrong in many different cultures.

An even more difficult problem for the person who wishes to dismiss morality as a mere product of culture is this: we cannot help comparing cultures and recognizing some cultural practices as morally superior. Think, for example, of ritual human sacrifice. This practice was common in many cultures at one time. Today most people probably know it only through movies like *Indiana Jones and the Temple of Doom*. People of just about every culture today see that this practice is wrong, hideously wrong. Even if some individual approves of it, it is still wrong. For anyone who makes a moral judgment of this sort, the conclusion is inescapable: the standard of morality has a reality deeper than culture.

Of course, our knowledge of the standard is transmitted by culture, and our understanding of the particulars of the standard is influenced by culture. But the standard itself must be deeper than that; otherwise the notion of moral progress would be impossible. For example, anyone who thinks that the abolition of slavery in the Western world was a good thing has really rejected cultural relativism. Anyone who is morally critical of any aspect of her own culture agrees that there is a standard higher than culture.

The rejection of cultural relativism should not be confused with *ethnocentrism,* the belief that one's own culture is morally superior to others. I can believe there is a moral standard higher than culture while recognizing that my own culture may fall short of that standard. And rejecting cultural relativism should not be equated with *moral dogmatism* either. The moral dogmatist believes his own moral views are infallible and is unwilling to consider the possibility that some of his own beliefs could need revising. If I truly believe in an objective moral standard, I should be open to the possibility that some of my own moral ideas need correcting.

Doubts about the Moral Law: Evolutionary Psychology

Another popular source of doubt about the objectivity of morality is the idea that morality can be explained by evolution. If this could really be done, it seems to me that it would say something very powerful about the origin of those natural processes that are described in evolution. But the fact is, nobody has the slightest idea how genuine moral laws, genuine "oughts," could be explained by evolution. Evolutionary psychologists or "sociobiologists" who try to explain morality invariably wind up explaining morality away. They do not explain why there are genuine moral laws; they only explain why humans (mistakenly) think there are.

It is conceivable that evolution could be used to explain various *instincts* or social *feelings*. But the moral order does not seem to consist of any such things. It is not an instinct, because it is itself the standard by which we judge our instincts to be good and bad. And it is not merely a social impulse or feeling. People who have dulled their consciences often are in fact obligated to do things, yet have no such feelings of obligation whatsoever. On the other hand, people with tender consciences often *feel* obligated to do things that no reasonable person would claim they really ought to do. Feelings and real obligations can't be identical.

In a similar way, one might by evolution try to explain why people who *believed* that they ought to treat their fellow humans decently might have been more likely to survive, and thus explain moral beliefs. But such a view cannot explain the *truth* of such beliefs. In other words, if I believe that evolution is the only foundation of morality, I have no reason to believe that moral obligations really hold. I only have a basis for believing that humans think they do.

But why shouldn't we accept the view that moral obligations

are not really objective? In a sense there is no proof that such a view is not correct, and certainly many people claim to think this way, and doubtless do think this way much of the time. However, when confronted with real moral evil — the horrors of genocide and child abuse, for example — it is hard to believe that moral judgments are just a biologically grounded illusion. However skeptical we may be about morality in theory, in practice we sense that human actions do matter. It is really right to care about people who are starving to death; it is really wrong to bomb school busses to achieve some political end.

Can Morality Be Naturalistically Explained?

But can't someone believe in morality without believing in God? Of course this is possible; many agnostics and atheists are deeply committed to moral ends. The question is whether such people have an adequate explanation of the moral truths they recognize. If there is no God, if the natural world is just a product of matter and time and chance, how did moral obligations arise?[2]

We have just seen that it is impossible to explain morality biologically by appealing to evolution. But is there some other natural explanation of morality that would make it unnecessary to bring God into the picture?

Certainly many naturalists have tried to explain morality. The fact that they have done so is one argument in favor of the objectivity of morality and against those who would reduce morality to culture or biology. Let us see how successful some of these attempts to explain morality as a natural fact are.

Someone who does not believe in God might try to explain moral obligations by viewing morality as a kind of social agreement or contract. There are many different versions of this idea,

---

2. The following section is strongly influenced by the argument of George Mavrodes in his article "Religion and The Queerness of Morality," in *Rationality, Religious Belief, and Moral Commitment,* ed. Robert Audi and William J. Wainwright (Ithaca, NY: Cornell University Press, 1986), 213-26.

but the core intuition is simply that in a society where individuals care only about themselves, life is likely to be "nasty, short, brutish, and poor," as philosopher Thomas Hobbes said. All of us need help at times; if we aren't willing to help others, then they are less likely to be willing to help us. So we will all be better off if we agree to certain rules of conduct, perhaps the kinds of rules that follow from the "golden rule" of doing unto others as you would have others do unto you. It is then in my own best interest to follow morality.

Such a social agreement view of morality certainly seems superior to the evolutionary view that explains away right and wrong altogether. However, I do not see how it could be an ultimately adequate account. The problem arises from the fact that on this view, morality rests in the end on self-interest. The social agreement theory says that I should be moral because in the long run I will be better off following that policy. This may be true for many people much of the time, but it is not always true.

Social theorists often call this problem the "free-rider" problem. Suppose it is true that all of us as a group will be better off if we all are moral. It does not follow from this fact that I as an individual will necessarily be better off. I might be better off if everyone else acts morally and I, on selective occasions when I am not likely to be caught, disregard morality and simply do what I wish or what I think will benefit me.

Think, for example, of the morality of cheating on a test. Probably society as a whole will be better off if people do not cheat on things like medical entrance exams; in that way, we will get better qualified physicians. But I may not be better off. Suppose that it is my dream to become a doctor and that the only way I can do so is by cheating.

One might object at this point that if I cheat, others may do so as well, and I will not really gain an advantage. However, others may cheat anyway, regardless of what I do. And if the others do not cheat, and I can do so without risk of getting caught, why should I not take advantage of the situation? I may be a "free-rider" who takes advantage of the fact that others are keeping the rules.

Many people say there is nothing wrong with this. They are the free-riders, who cheat on income taxes, or to use a less clear-cut

moral case, listen to public television and radio without ever con-
tributing. So long as enough other people pay their taxes to keep
the system going, and contribute enough to keep the stations
funded, it would seem that a free-rider is in fact better off.

If we couple the free-rider attitude with the cynical belief that
others will act the same way, then the golden rule is converted to
the notorious bumper-sticker philosophy "Do it to the others
before they can do it to you." At this point morality has been
abandoned. In the end, if we believe that the attitude of the
free-rider is morally wrong, then we must believe that morality
has some foundation deeper than mere self-interest. Self-interested
social agreement cannot be the foundation of morality because the
fundamental moral principle that one ought to keep one's agree-
ments must be presupposed by any such social contract.

Conscience: God's Calling Card

Moral obligations are facts, facts we can feel or fail to feel, facts
we can be right about or mistaken about. However, they are
facts of a peculiar kind. Ordinary people have for millennia
experienced these facts as fundamental clues to the nature of the
universe. They have sensed that the experience of "oughtness"
shows that the Mind or Intelligence, whatever it is, that lies
behind the universe is a Moral Being, a Being concerned about
right and wrong. They have regarded the voice of conscience as
the voice of God. It is, to be sure, a voice that is sometimes
clouded and distorted by the voice of culture. However, culture
can transmit truth as well as error. Though each individual's
understanding of the standard (including my own, of course)
may be faulty at points, still we hear enough to know there is a
standard that is independent of ourselves and that we do not
always live up to.

If God exists, nothing is more natural than that we should
experience a moral "ought." Without God the moral order would
be a strange kind of inexplicable brute fact. How could there be
an objective law with no lawgiver? If there is a God, what better

calling card could he have left in us than the consciousness of the moral order? At bottom our obligations to be kind, loving, and just are obligations to respect the value of persons.

Some people who do not believe in God have tried to explain morality as being rooted in human nature. Certain ways of living together seem to fit with our nature; when we live in those ways we flourish. When we live immorally, we shrivel up and become less than we should be. This is probably the best way to view morality if someone does not believe in God. However, the idea of a common human nature seems increasingly to be rejected by those who do not believe in a God who created human beings "of one blood," to use the language of the Bible. And even if we can accept a common human nature, such a view still seems to presuppose just what needs explaining: why human persons possess inherent value and dignity.

If God is real, then personhood is no mere "surface phenomenon" in the universe, a late and accidental outcome of atoms in motion. In the traditional Jewish and Christian view, God himself is personal, the supreme person. Persons are what the universe is all about. If, then, the supreme reality and source of all value is a person, other persons should be respected because they are made in his image. Such values as the equality of all humans and the need for compassion towards the weak and the sick make sense. All people are created in God's image, and thus all reflect something of God's own value. All people have a right to life, liberty, and the pursuit of happiness. Such a right is not merely given by the state; it is a fundamental right the state ought to protect, and the existence of such a right must be understood as a consequence of the status of human persons as creatures made in the image of God. Those who are sick deserve care, whether or not they can make a "social contribution," simply because they are persons.

This does not mean that obligations to human persons are all there is to morality. If the natural world is God's creation, then it too is to be treated with respect, including the animals who are also God's creatures. In the Judeo-Christian view, humans are given the status of stewards of the natural order, responsible ultimately to a personal God for what they do with God's creation. If we recognize that the value of personhood lies then at the center of all moral obligations, then we must also recognize that morality provides a crucial clue to the meaning of the universe.

What Do These Clues Mean?

I have tried to show how the experience of the moral order in the universe supports the Christian conception of God. One should not conclude from this, however, that this clue alone, even together with the clues discussed in the last chapter, shows the truth of Christianity. We are still far from the God of Abraham, Isaac, and Jacob, and even further from showing that Jesus is God's supreme revelation to us humans.

Nevertheless, I have tried to show that a belief in the kind of God Christians believe in is far from unreasonable. There are three profound mysteries that are pervasive in human experience. The mystery of cosmic wonder is felt in the strange way humans experience the universe as a "might-never-have-been." The mystery of purposive order is felt as we perceive the value produced by the order of nature and strongly suggests that there is mind at the root of the universe. The mystery of a moral order, felt in the experience of "oughtness," conveys to us an objectively real order of rightness and wrongness.

All of these mysteries are what Peter Berger calls "*signals of transcendence* within the . . . human condition."[3] They can plausibly be seen as clues pointing to the reality of a being with many of the characteristics of the Christian God. Christianity says that God is the creator of the universe, the reason why a universe that might-never-have-been exists. God is the mind who provides the order and structure that pervades the physical universe. Finally, God is seen by Christianity as the supreme person, who provides a moral order to that same universe by creating persons in his image and commanding those persons to respect the dignity and worth of persons and their creations, human and divine.

3. Peter Berger, *A Rumor of Angels* (Garden City, NY: Doubleday, 1970), 52.

Each of these clues has exactly the characteristics one would expect to find in the calling cards a God would leave of himself. They permeate human experience and are discernible by anyone, regardless of the person's degree of education or sophistication. Nevertheless, they are in no way coercive. A person must have a certain degree of sensitivity and openness to God properly to read and interpret the clues.

Suppose that Jim from Chapter One has had his attention directed to these mysteries and thereby has had some "suspicions" raised. He at least now thinks it possible that God exists. Where should he look for further clues? The most plausible place to look is at ourselves. If a supreme person exists, and has made human persons in his own image, as Christianity claims, then human personhood deserves a more careful look. If there are more clues to be found, that is a promising place to look for them. We shall therefore turn in the next chapter to the fundamental mysteries that are posed by our own being as human persons.

CHAPTER SIX

The Mystery of Persons

What a chimera then is man! What a novelty! What a monster, what a chaos, what a contradiction, what a prodigy! Judge of all things, imbecile worn of the earth; depository of truth, a sink of uncertainty and error; the pride and refuse of the universe!

Pascal, *Pensées*

I don't see myself as so much dust that has appeared in the world but as a being that was expected, prefigured, called forth. In short, as a being that could, it seems, come only from a creator; and this idea of a creating hand that created me refers me back to God.

Jean Paul Sartre,
Interview with Simone de Beauvoir

HUMAN BEINGS HAVE always been puzzled about themselves. Socrates is reputed to have abandoned astronomy because he thought it was odd to try to learn about the stars when he did not even know his own self. Socrates found his own nature to be paradoxical. He could not decide if he was a creature akin to a monster or a being with a "simpler, gentler nature, partaking of something divine."[1]

Since the days of Socrates we have learned a great deal about the stars, but it is doubtful that we know more than Socrates about ourselves. If we care to look, there is much to see; the difficulty lies in making sense of what is seen. The same ambiguity Socrates saw in himself is still present in us. The morning newspaper that includes stories of astounding heroism, brilliant ingenuity, and selfless devotion also recounts the most sickening and degrading actions imaginable. Human potential seems boundless, but the cartoon character Pogo said it best: "We have met the enemy and he is us."

Yet even our evil deeds in some ways point to our greatness. Crabs and toads aren't capable of great wickedness. Only a creature with self-consciousness and freedom can be really evil. A deeper look at the total message of human nature seems amply justified.

Christians believe that human persons are not simply a part of the created order, but a special part of that order. Two things are special about us.

First, we are created in the image and likeness of God. This means that we have the capacity to be like God, to reflect his character. To be sure, Christianity balances this claim that we are created in God's image with the claim that we have rebelled against God. This rebellion, called *sin*, is bound to disturb the likeness between us and God. Still, if Christianity is true, then we should possess some unique "godlike" characteristics, even if they are distorted.

The second special thing about us, according to Christianity, is that we were created to enjoy a special relationship with God. We were made to know and enjoy God and cannot truly fulfill our destiny apart from him. Once more, the fact of our sinfulness qualifies this claim. Though we need God and cannot truly be happy without him, we are usually far from understanding this. Instead, we constantly run away from God and try to replace him with substitutes.

1. *Phaedrus,* 230a.

Still, if Christianity is true, certain characteristics should be present in human *nature* and in human *desires*. Let us look more closely at each of these two areas, and see what we find. Those areas of human experience should provide us with keys, if there are keys to be found. We need to look closely at any keys we find and see if they "fit the lock."

Dust of the Earth and Stewards of Nature

The paradoxical character of human nature has many dimensions. On the one hand we are products of nature, and on the other hand we transcend nature. We are in many ways the outcome of factors we have no control over. Each of us is born with a particular set of parents, in a particular physical and cultural environment. We are endowed with a particular genetic structure, which in turn determines a host of factors, including sex, height, range of potential intelligence, and so on. Each of these potentials is in turn affected by the environment in ways too complicated to understand fully. The end result is a creature who is the joint product of nature and nurture, with the two factors interacting to such a degree that the debate over which is more important becomes almost unsolvable.

A story similar to the above can be told about many species of animals. But in the case of human beings, there is more to the story. Each of us is certainly a product of nature, but each of us is certainly more than a product. For we possess imagination and the power of reflective choice. These capacities enable us to become, at least in part, producers and not mere products, creatures who are also creators.

Consider the power of imagination. To be able to imagine is to be able to escape from the prison of actuality. In imagination we think not only about what actually exists, but about what *could* but does not yet exist. We can think not merely of the past, but about the future; not merely about what we have done, but about what we could do.

Often our imaginations serve us by allowing us to escape

from our actual circumstances. I sit in a heated room in grey, cold, wintery west Michigan. In my imagination I can frolic on the beach in warm, sunny Florida. I can escape from a dull or painful present by pulling a favorite novel off the shelf and entering another world.

Imagination, however, is thankfully not a mere escape valve. It is the power to conceive new and better futures. It means we are not locked into repeating the past; we can think of new possibilities.

And we don't just have the power to imagine alternative actions; we can freely choose between these alternatives. All of us make such choices constantly. All of us know that we have this freedom and that we are responsible for our use of it.

Or at least we think we do. But do we really have this freedom? Determinists would claim that our experience of freedom is an illusion. We do not really transcend the natural order. Each and every human action is determined by the laws of nature; we are just as determined as anything else in nature.

Is the determinist right? We must begin by noting that here the determinist's frequent appeal to science is illegitimate. It may be that scientists must presuppose determinism as a working hypothesis. But the claim that everything is actually determined is not a scientific conclusion but a philosophical assumption. The question concerns the limits of science, which is not a question *within* science but a question *about* science.

Second, no one has actually discovered the scientific laws that the determinists believe underlie all human behavior. Though several generations of psychologists, sociologists, and social scientists of other stripes have labored mightily, no one knows laws of human behavior that are in any way comparable to the laws discovered by the physical sciences. Social scientists discover statistical correlations that hold in a probabilistic manner for limited groups of people for limited amounts of time. They learn, for example, that children who are abused are more likely to become child abusers, or that teenagers are more likely to buy shampoo if it is sold in a particular colored container.

Such probabilistic generalizations are very useful. An advertiser, for example, using this sort of information, can calculate the effectiveness of a certain type of ad that is being run for a certain income group in a particular country. But no one even pretends to be able to make precise predictions, on the basis of this sort of information, about the behavior of particular individuals in real-life situations.

Of course most social scientists don't admit that people have genuine freedom. (Though one political scientist has said that people have "quasi-free will"; they behave [surprise] just as they would if they really did have free will![2]) They usually take refuge in the claim that the determining laws exist but are too complicated to discover. This, however, is purely an expression of faith on their part and gains no credit from the genuine achievements of science. So the sciences provide no good reason to deny human freedom. But is there any good reason to accept it?

The most compelling reason to believe in freedom is simply that each one of us in practice is aware of our freedom and responsibility. It is easy enough to deny freedom of choice when we are theorizing, when we adopt the attitude of spectators. But just as is the case with morality, it is quite another thing to deny the reality of freedom when we are *living*.

Life is a series of choices. No one can live without considering alternatives, without asking which of the possible alternatives is *best,* which one *ought* I to choose. But I cannot even begin to consider which act I should perform unless I presuppose that I really do have a choice. If all my acts are determined, it might make sense for me to try to predict or guess what I will do, but it would make no sense to try to *decide* what I should do. Life is not a day at the racetrack where we sit back and bet on our own "race" as if we were spectators of ourselves. Even the most dogmatic determinist implicitly believes in freedom every time he or she is faced with the necessity of making a responsible choice!

Human freedom is of course limited in many ways. Our options are always finite, and they are often weighted. People cannot choose apart from their past. But when we praise and blame others and when we recognize our own responsibility for our choices, we clearly show that we know we are not simply helpless

---

2. Michael Lessnoff, *The Structure of Social Science* (London: Allen and Unwin, 1974), 65.

victims in life. We are products of nature, but we are also responsible choosers.

How is this human capacity for freedom to be explained? How is it that creatures who are obviously a part of nature can also partially transcend nature?

A Christian answers these questions by claiming that human beings are that part of nature that reflects a reality deeper than nature. We can partially transcend nature because we are made in the image of the one who is totally transcendent of nature. We are creative beings with the power of free choice because we were made in the likeness of the person who created the whole of nature by a free choice.

Of course many people have used this power of choice in dreadful ways. And in some ways this misuse of freedom diminishes and destroys freedom. If we continually give in to an evil impulse, eventually we lose the ability to resist at all. Christianity teaches that in a mysterious way the whole human race has done something like this. We have — freely — given in to evil and have become "slaves to sin." This is a condition that we cannot set right just by making a New Year's resolution or by turning over a new leaf. But this "bondage to evil" does not mean human freedom is an illusion. It rather means that God takes our freedom so seriously that he allows our actions to produce their full consequences.

So, on the whole, human beings look pretty much as they should if Christianity is true. The key of human nature we have found opens at least one lock. We are free beings who partially transcend nature, though we have terribly misused our freedom. Such freedom is hard for a naturalist to explain. If human persons are a product of an impersonal material universe, then it seems impossible for humans to transcend that impersonal universe. However, if the universe itself is the product of a transcendent person, then it is not surprising that human persons partially reflect their transcendent origins.

Please notice that this point in no way hinges on the question as to whether God created human beings by a "special act" or through a process of evolution. The point is that nature contains something that transcends itself, something we would not expect nature to produce if nature existed "on its own." If human beings have been produced by natural processes, then those natural processes are evidently guided by a purposive design. If nature can produce something that transcends nature, then this says something surprising about nature.

Responsible freedom by no means exhausts the image of God in man. Essentially the same point could have been made by focusing on creativity or rationality. The point is that besides the calling cards God has left in nature and in the moral order, he has left one fundamental clue to his reality, which gives every one of us who has any degree of self-knowledge a chance to discover him. That clue is ourselves. Perhaps Pogo should also have said, "We have found a clue to the universe, and it is us."

The Need to Believe

At the beginning of this chapter we noted that two things about human beings must be special if Christianity is true. First, we must have some special godlike characteristics, for we are made in God's image.

Second, since God made us for a special purpose that includes loving fellowship with himself, we must in some way need God. We should desire to know him. Or at least we must be constituted in such a way that we cannot find ultimate peace and fulfillment apart from him.

Is this the case? Indeed it looks like it is. Down through the ages human beings have been incurably religious. The urge to believe in and worship a "higher power" is present in virtually every human culture.

Someone might cite Communist countries as proof that human beings can live without their gods. But religious faith thrived in Russia during its Communist period. It now appears that despite decades of persecution, the Christian church in China multiplied under Communism. And before claiming that Communist societies, past and present, are truly "secular" we ought to ponder carefully the extent to which Marxism itself can function like a religion, replete with veneration of the tombs of "saints" such as Lenin.

Usually, however, the skeptic will admit that religious needs are prevalent but reject the idea that this says something deep about human nature. The existence of these religious urges is explained by various natural factors. The skeptic in fact tries to argue that these natural needs to believe are sufficient to explain religious belief away. The fact that people need to believe in God is a sign that God is an illusion. The whole business is wish fulfillment; God is a crutch for the weak, an indulgence for people with a flabby intellectual conscience.

This widespread assumption that the need to believe in God discredits religious belief is really remarkable. It takes a fact that must be true if God is real and has made humans to fellowship with himself and tries to count that fact as evidence *against* God's reality!

Suppose that it is true that human beings have a fundamental psychological need to believe in and worship a God. Should this be interpreted as a sign that faith in God is suspicious in nature because it is likely to be a product of wish fulfillment? Or should it be interpreted as verifying the existence of a "God-shaped hole" in human nature, a hole implanted by God himself?

Critics often remark in this context that the existence of a need does not guarantee that it will be satisfied. A shipwrecked sailor on a life raft may have a desperate need and a burning desire for pure water. He may want it so badly that he hallucinates its reality. Clearly this doesn't mean there is water available to him. Likewise, a person may need or want God, but God may not be there for her or anyone.

Notice, however, that the analogy breaks down. The sailor as an individual may not get any water, but it would be very odd if he had this need and water did not exist.[3] The fact that people in general have a need for water is strong evidence that there is such a thing as water, though this does not imply that an individual

3. This point was made clearly and effectively by C. S. Lewis in "The Weight of Glory," in *The Weight of Glory and Other Addresses* (Grand Rapids: Wm. B. Eerdmans, 1965), 6.

person will get water on any specific occasion. In a similar manner, the fact that we have a deep need to believe in and find God strongly suggests that God is real, though of course this does not mean that any one of us will actually discover God and establish a relationship with him. It would be very odd indeed if we had a fundamental need for something that did not exist.

The Craving for Eternity

Up to this point we have talked in general terms about a religious need, or a need for God or gods. What is this need (or these needs) like, in more specific terms? What are the contours of the "God-shaped hole"? This need shows itself in three primary dimensions that are closely related. These are the desire for eternal life, the desire for eternal meaning, and the desire for eternal love.

The desire for *eternal life* is the most evident manifestation of the need for God. Burial mounds of the most primitive societies show that from time immemorial people have longed for life beyond the grave. Today we still share that longing. The theme song for the TV program *Fame* included the chorus, "I want to live forever." But now many of us lack the robust confidence of previous societies that the longing will be satisfied.

What could be more natural than death? Every human being will die; every member of every animal species will die. Yet what is more unnatural than death? I remember clearly my own mother's death. In one sense it was perfectly natural, yet in the most profound way it seemed and still seems to me an outrage. How strange that we never experience death without seeing it as a breach, an intrusion into the way things ought to be. Yet we have never experienced things any other way, and in truth we can't even imagine how the current natural order, with its delicate ecology, could go on without death. Yet deep in our hearts we feel death should not be, was not meant to be.

The second dimension of our craving for eternity is the desire for *eternal meaning*. One of the most troubling things about time is the way it robs our activities of their meaning. Who has not looked at the wreck of ancient civilizations, buried beyond memory, and wondered what purpose was served by the stupendous labors of those millions of people? I have often wondered whether in two hundred years anyone will care about anything I have done, or even know that I have lived. Yet all of us want our lives to have a meaning that lasts; we want it so badly that the ephemeral character of our achievements threatens to undo the meaningfulness they actually possess.

This second dimension deepens our understanding of the first. For it reveals that the eternal life we want is not merely an extension of the present. It is a different *kind* of life, a life in which one activity would not merely be followed by another, a life in which our activities would have depth and thickness. We want our lives to possess a meaning and value that is solid and impervious to the vagaries of time and chance. We want lives that are eternally meaningful.

What would such a life be like? We do not know in any clear or definite way, but surely the deepest clue we have is the love of one person for another. Everyone knows that "love makes the world go round"; everyone craves love and feels at bottom that it is the most important thing in life. Yet earthly love, even when it is happy and fortunate, does not satisfy our deepest urges. This is not to say that earthly loves are not rich and valuable. It is not to say that romantic love is not tingly, nor that married love cannot be rich and warm.

Strangely enough, even in our most happy and treasured moments of love, we often feel something is missing. We find ourselves wanting more but not knowing what is the more we want. As Aldous Huxley once said, "There comes a time when one says, even of Shakespeare, even of Beethoven, 'Is that all?'" We are anxious and subtly distressed, even when — especially when — we experience moments we know should be the happiest ones in our lives.

Why is this so? We crave eternity, and earthly loves resemble eternity enough to kindle our deepest love. Yet earthly loves are not eternal. (Though they can be *made* eternal, transformed by being taken up into eternity.) Our sense that love is the clue to what it's all about is right on target, but earthly love itself merely points us in the right direction.

What we want is an *eternal love*, a love that loves us uncon-
ditionally, accepts us as we are, while helping us to become all we
can become. We want a love that is not subject to fortune and
fate, a love in which we can be fully known and fully appreciated.
We want a love that cares enough about us to want our best, a
love that knows what is good and is hard enough to seek it, not
merely a sloppy sentimental love that would gratify our whims
and capricious urges.

In short, we want *God*, the God of Christian faith. He is the
suitor who courts us, the one who is love and who loves with a
terrible abandon. He is the one who loves for time and eternity,
fixed and unshakable in his purposes, totally unselfish in his desires
for us. Such a love would give our lives meaning, and such an
ongoing life of love is what we crave in our hope that death is not
the final word.

Thus we see that God has hardly left us bereft of clues to his
reality and character. If for some reason we are blind to the
mysteries of the universe, we should still see the mystery of our
own being. And when we are not reflective enough to see God in
the mystery of our own being, he is still evident in one thing we
can hardly miss: the deepest desires of our own hearts. The hard
part is not finding the clues, but deciding to trust what we find.

CHAPTER SEVEN

The Divine Suitor

I fled Him, down the nights and down the days;
  I fled Him, down the arches of the years;
I fled Him, down the labyrinthine ways
    Of my own mind; and in the mist of tears
I hid from Him, and under running laughter.
      Up vistaed hopes I sped;
      And shot, precipitated,
Adown Titanic glooms of chasmed fears,
  From those strong Feet that followed, followed after.
      But with unhurrying chase,
      And unperturbed pace,
  Deliberate speed, majestic instancy,
      They beat — and a Voice beat
      More instant than the Feet —
"All things betray thee, who betrayest Me."

          Francis Thompson, *The Hound of Heaven*

IMAGINE TWO SCHOOLCHILDREN are studying the American political system. Both are supposed to write a report on a former president. Jerry pulls out his encyclopedia and begins to list all the relevant facts: the state the president was born in, previous offices held, positions on issues, major accomplishments in office. Boring, he thinks.

Jan is both more ingenious and more fortunate. Since the former president lives in the same state, she has herself driven to his hometown, where she tours the nearby presidential library, and much to her surprise bumps into the man himself as she walks out of the building. Having the presence of mind to introduce herself and explain her mission, she soon finds herself talking with the great man in his private office, hearing him tell stories about the crises in his administration and great events he had helped to shape. As Jan listens she finds her enthusiasm for politics and the drama of political decision making growing. She is filled with admiration for the man she is speaking to, both for his accomplishments and for his kindness in spending time with her. Incredible, she thinks.

There is a profound difference between knowing about a person and knowing a person. The difference is not the information the two students have. Jerry may know the same facts as Jan, but Jan has met the man himself.

Knowing about someone is often very useful; even Jan needed to know enough about the former president to find his library and to recognize him when she saw him. But actually encountering a person, getting to know him or her as one person to another, is a completely different type of experience. It puts our knowledge in a completely different framework.

So far in this book we have focused on knowing *about* God. We have looked at the clues to God's reality to be found in nature, in the moral order, in the human self, and in our deepest desires as humans. These clues make it possible for an individual to know about God in at least a vague kind of way. Such "knowing about" is not to be despised. It has its value, especially in the right context. But that context is discovered not in knowing still more facts about God, but in a knowledge of God himself.

In the previous chapter the final clue to God's reality we examined was our own desire for God. That desire is a desire for God, not simply a desire for knowledge about God. Can our desire be met? Can we encounter God?

The Lover Appears

If God is real and has made us to know and experience him, then certainly there must be a way for us to find him. This is the assumption that underlay our look at the clues God has strewn about in the natural order and in the human self. I called these clues God's calling cards. A calling card is of course not an end in itself. It is a sign that someone has called on us and may call again. We should then be on the lookout, not merely for more clues, but for God himself. And for the person who has met God, the calling cards may look insignificant indeed.

Though we still of course use business cards, the old custom of "calling cards" is practically extinct today. However, there was a time when someone who called on a friend did indeed leave such a card. If the friend was more than a friend, then more than a card might be left. In those days a man courting a woman might leave flowers, a note, a book of poems. Such things are still known to happen in our own day, though in these times the woman may be doing the courting! And such gestures are not without meaning. But if the person courted returns the love of the lover, such reminders will pale in significance when compared to the chance to feel the lover's touch, to hear the lover's voice, and to speak together with the lover about their own deepest feelings.

For us to gain knowledge *about* God, God had to take the initiative. He had to plant the clues and give us the ability to discern those clues. How much more will we be dependent on God if we are to know him and not just know about him! How could we possibly have a personal relation with God if God himself did not take the initiative?

It is the stupendous claim of Christianity that God has done just that. In the Bible God is seen as the divine suitor, faithfully loving and seeking to woo an often faithless group of creatures. In the Old Testament, God creates and courts a special people for himself, a people who would know and serve him, and through whom he would ultimately make contact with all his rebellious creatures. Throughout the Old Testament, God is portrayed as a faithful, loving husband, as well as an ardent suitor. Though Israel constantly goes astray, God is constantly seeking her out, warning her of the unhappiness caused by idolatrous substitutes for the deepest human need. He entices her with the promises of blessing and satisfaction that go with ardent love of one's Creator. Through prophets and priests God displays his love and calls his people to himself.

This long courtship culminates for Christians in Jesus Christ. In Jesus what was already suggested by Isaiah and other Old Testament prophets becomes crystal clear: God's beloved does not consist only of the Jewish people. Rather, through Jesus, the son of David, God is creating a community from all of humankind, a community in which there will be neither Jew nor Greek, male nor female, black nor white. Jesus not only announces God's love, he embodies it. Jesus does not merely tell us God is our suitor; he is himself the suitor!

In Jesus God showed what kind of a suitor he is, and he showed us what kind of love motivates his wooing. The most powerful love is the love that gives itself for the lover, the love that sacrifices itself for the other. Jesus represents this love in its purest form, not merely in words but in deeds. The very idea of God becoming a human being entails giving up the riches of divinity for the finitude and hardships of mortality. And what a human life it is: born in poverty, living among the poor and downtrodden, and culminating in a shameful, painful death!

And why? One of the greatest Christian thinkers, Søren Kierkegaard, tells a story to answer this question.[1] Suppose a mighty king fell in love with a simple, humble maiden. How should he court her? Should he order her to love him on pain of imprisonment if she does not? Even if the woman submits, such a fearful response could hardly be called love, nor would it satisfy the king.

Should the king shower her with dazzling gifts and throw stupendous balls in her honor? In that case, how could the king know if it was himself the girl cared about or rather his riches and power? How could she get to know him, and he her?

No, the best solution is for the king to put aside his rank and riches, and to woo the woman in disguise. Only in this way can

---

1. See Søren Kierkegaard, *Philosophical Fragments,* rev. ed. (Princeton, NJ: Princeton University Press, 1962), 28-45.

she get to know him as a person. If he is truly kingly and truly loving, he will be willing not merely to take on the disguise of the peasant; he will be willing to sacrifice his comfort and rank altogether if it should be necessary to win her love.

Such a love can hardly be grasped, even in imagination. Yet in his willingness to sacrifice his throne for his love, the king would reveal himself as truly loving. His love and his character would be seen not merely in words but in his life.

The difference between a king and a peasant maiden is of course merely a jest in comparison with the difference between a creature and its creator. Yet in Jesus, God comes to us on our level. He does not merely adopt humanness as a disguise. He actually takes on our humanness, shares our joys and sorrows. He lives a life for others and dies a death for all of us. For only in this way could we see clearly the self-giving love that is God's very nature.

God is a determined suitor. Despite the obstacles we humans throw up, he is in the process of winning a people, a bride for himself. The victorious, powerful character of God's love in Jesus will not allow Jesus to remain in the grave. Jesus rises from the dead and in doing so announces once more, not merely in words but in deed, that God's love is eternal. Our deepest need — the need for an eternal life of love — can be satisfied. If we trust the divine suitor, Jesus, we can become part of the joyous community of God's beloved. We can become sons and daughters of the most high, citizens in the kingdom of God. Our rebelliousness and the death that is the outcome of that rebelliousness are overcome.

The Uniqueness of Christianity

The preceding is a sketch, ever so fragmentary and full of gaps, of what Christians believe God has done to make it possible for humans to know him. The story sounds good, perhaps too good to be true. What reasons do we have for thinking it is true? After all, many religions claim that they possess a word from God. What reason is there to believe the Christian story?

Perhaps it is reasonable to think that God would reveal him-

self in some special way so that humans could get to know him
and not just know about him. But why should one think that he
has done this in Jesus, rather than in the Buddha or Muhammad
or Confucius?

First of all, Christians do not necessarily claim that God has
revealed himself *solely* in Jesus. God has spoken through Moses
and the Old Testament prophets. Even in the Old Testament, God
is seen as having representatives in other peoples than the Jews.[2]
Many people today, both in and outside of Christianity, claim to
have had mystical experiences in which they have become aware
of God. Others may in fact be responding to God's voice without
even recognizing that it is God who inspires their endeavors. Christians do not deny that there are many true insights in other religions and that God is the source of all truth.

What Christians claim is that God has revealed himself *decisively* in Jesus, that it is in Jesus that we get the clearest and truest
account of God. Jesus provides us with a picture of God so sharp
that it becomes the standard, the key by which all others are judged
and interpreted.

Ultimately all the rest of a Christian's beliefs hang on this
belief in Jesus. The belief that God has forgiven sins is bound up
with the belief that Jesus is the "lamb of God who takes away the
sins of the world." The belief that Christians will rise from the
dead is based on Jesus' resurrection. Even the belief that the Bible
is God's word rests on a trust in Jesus — the acceptance of Jesus'
attitude toward the Old Testament and a belief that the New
Testament was written by followers of Jesus who were endowed
by him with special authority. All the other doctrines also revolve
around Jesus.

The reason this is so is that Jesus is seen not merely as a wise
man who knows a lot about God, or even as a prophet with a
special message from God. Jesus is God himself. He is the divine
suitor.

---

2. See the story of Balaam (Num. 22-24) for a prime example. Though
Balaam did not serve the Lord with a pure heart and though he ultimately came
to a bad end, it is clear he was a true prophet of God who "spoke the word of
the Lord."

For better or worse this claim marks Christianity off from other religions. Followers of Islam do not view Muhammad as divine; Muhammad is a prophet of God, and to say more is blasphemy. Jews would never consider the idea that Abraham or Moses were divine. The best historical accounts of the Buddha make it clear that he did not consider himself to be divine, nor did his early followers; the Buddha was a wise man who had reached Enlightenment. Confucius is also seen as a wise teacher, never as a divine savior.

The closest parallel to the Christian conviction that Jesus is God incarnate would appear to be the Hindu notion of an *avatar.* Many Hindus believe that particular men and women are special incarnations of divinity. A similar idea is found in later Mahayana Buddhism. But both these Hindu and Buddhist parallels regard the *avatars* or the incarnations of "Buddha-hood" as plural. There have been many *avatars,* and there can be many more. Christians believe, however, that Jesus is God's "only begotten son." He is not merely one in a series of appearances of God or one among many manifestations of God. He is God himself.

It is this claim that sets Christianity apart. One cannot simply view Christianity as "one true religion among many true religions." Christianity is either true in a unique way or it is not true at all. Anyone who takes Christianity seriously is forced to wrestle with this bold, even brash, claim. To wrestle with this claim is essentially to wrestle with the person of Jesus. Who was he? Who is he?

CHAPTER EIGHT

Was Jesus Really God?

Faith is not blind. . . . In the case of Christian faith it arose for the earliest disciples from historical contemporaneity with Jesus. They were not *compelled* by the evidence: plenty of people saw it and declined to commit themselves. But the evidence was the ground on which they committed themselves.

Michael Green, *The Truth of God Incarnate*

Signs are taken for wonders. "We would see a sign!" The word within word, unable to speak a word, swaddled with darkness. In the juvescence of the year came Christ the tiger.

T. S. Eliot, from *Gerontion*

IN THE 1960s Thomas Howard wrote *Christ the Tiger*. In this book he shows very powerfully how frequently people, even professing Christians, manage to construct a Jesus who will fit their own needs and preconceptions. They do not want to face the actual Jesus, who is no tame kitty, but a troublesome tiger.

The tendency Howard wrote about is a perennial temptation. The figure of Jesus looms so powerfully in the minds of people —

even the minds of non-Christians — that it is hard to resist making Jesus into the patron saint of whatever cause we feel most deeply about. Intellectual honesty, however, demands that a person who is interested in Jesus make a serious attempt to listen to the actual Jesus of history. There is little value in wrestling with a Jesus who exists only in our own imagination.

Searching for the Actual Jesus

But can the Jesus of history be known? He lived a long time ago, and almost all our knowledge of him comes from the Bible. Can this be a trustworthy source of information?

Christians of course believe that the Bible is reliable, since they think it is a book that humans produced under the inspiration of God. But one cannot expect people who are not already Christians to accept such a view of the Bible.

Let us put aside, then, as question-begging, any assumption that the Bible is inspired by God. (Of course it would be equally question-begging to assume that the Bible is an ordinary human book that God had no role in producing.) Let us simply decide to treat the Bible as a historical document. Though many Christians believe the Bible is inspired and even infallible, properly interpreted, we need not consider such questions here. Our question is simply whether the New Testament picture of Jesus, taken as a whole, is basically truthful.

Now there seems to be little question that the New Testament represents Jesus as divine. His birth is miraculous; a virgin is said to be impregnated by the Spirit of God. His public ministry includes many stupendous miracles that could only be due to God and that therefore show at least that God was at work in his life: the blind and the lame are healed; thousands are fed from a tiny amount of food; Jesus himself walks on a lake and stills a raging storm on command. Jesus himself makes claims to divinity. He uses titles that connote divinity and claims he has the authority to forgive sins. He predicts his own execution and resurrection and then fulfills the prediction. His followers go on to claim that he is divine and that his life, death, and resurrection are God's provision for saving the human race.

So a reasonable person can hardly deny that the historical records we have do represent Jesus as divine. Many people, however, including many scholars, are inclined to be skeptical about the historical reliability of the New Testament. It is commonly thought that the miracle stories and claims to divinity must be later interpolations added by pious followers. On this view Jesus was a wonderful moral teacher who was persecuted and eventually executed for his courageous teachings. The stories of divinity were understandable attempts by prescientific folk to give Jesus' teachings the authority they deserve.

Often the reasoning behind this view simply begs the question of Jesus' divinity. A skeptic reasons that miracles just *can't* happen and an individual human being just *can't* be divine. So the miracles and claims to divinity *must* have been added later.

It is interesting to note that the people who first put forward this idea originally assumed that the New Testament must have been written quite a long time after the events. After all, it would seem to take time for legends to develop and be added to eyewitness accounts. However, the best scholars today, whether Christian or not, are agreed that the New Testament was written quite soon after Jesus' life.[1] Some epistles of Paul are accepted by nearly everyone as the earliest parts, and these were written at the latest only twenty to thirty years after Jesus' death. Already in these epistles the tradition of Jesus' divinity seems well established. And the Gospels themselves were written only a few years after this, far sooner than the gap of several generations originally postulated by those who saw Jesus' divinity as a later myth.

It is also worth noting that the New Testament compares very favorably in these respects with other historical documents from antiquity. The New Testament is written closer in time to the events reported, and the texts that have been preserved are both more numerous and earlier than is the case with other ancient docu-

---

1. For a good telling of the story of how early dates for the New Testament came to be accepted, see Stephen Neill and N. T. Wright, *The Interpretation of the New Testament 1861–1968*, 2nd ed. (Oxford: Oxford University Press, 1988).

ments. Of course this does not mean that the New Testament is necessarily historically reliable, but it does suggest that its historical testimony should be seriously considered.

Some skeptics claim that the Gospels do not purport to record history; rather, they were meant as pious myths and legends. But this does not seem a plausible claim. The evidence against this lies simply in *reading* the Gospels. They just don't read like myths. The Oxford English don C. S. Lewis, who was very much at home in the field of mythology, has this telling comment:

> I have been reading poems, romances, vision literature, legends, myths all my life. I know what they are like. I know that none of them is like this [the New Testament record]. Of this text there are only two possible views. Either this is re-portage — though it may no doubt contain errors — pretty close to the facts; nearly as close as Boswell. Or else, some unknown writer in the second century, without known predecessors or successors, suddenly anticipated the whole technique of modern, novelistic, realistic narrative. If it is untrue, it must be narrative of that kind.[2]

Lewis is here claiming that the idea that the New Testament picture of Jesus is a late "mythological" distortion of the "real Jesus" (who was a simple moral teacher) will not hold water. As *literature* the Gospels don't fit the genre of "myth," even if the story is one that has mythlike power. It is a *realistic narrative,* a narrative that has a history-like feel.[3] It purports to be a historical account of Jesus, one that has good credentials, an account of a man who claimed to be divine and performed miracles and was regarded as divine by his earliest, eyewitness followers. We may reject this Jesus and the testimony of his followers. But we ought not delude ourselves into thinking that we are rejecting the "Jesus of myth" in favor of "the real Jesus." For "the real Jesus" we

2. C. S. Lewis, "Modern Theology and Biblical Criticism," in *Christian Reflections* (London: Geoffrey Bles, 1967), 155.

3. The theologian who has done most to develop this understanding of the Gospel narratives is Hans Frei. See his *The Eclipse of Biblical Narrative* (New Haven: Yale University Press, 1974).

want to accept is invariably our own creation. It is not a response
to the evidence as we have it.

Of course the fact that the New Testament appears to be
historical testimony does not mean that it is historically reliable.
Lots of people have written unreliable histories. Plenty of people
reject the New Testament. Still, it is important to recognize that
it *is* testimony. The New Testament makes certain claims, and
while people are free to disagree with those claims, they are not
free to misrepresent the nature of the claims themselves.

There is of course a whole scholarly industry that has developed to try to recover "the historical Jesus." Scholars engaged in
this quest have looked at the Gospels in the New Testament as
well as other noncanonical writings. Complicated theories have
been developed about how the New Testament came into existence,
including much speculation about the order in which the books
were written, what sources the writers may have had to draw on,
the situations in which the books were written, and so on. Some
of these theories seem somewhat probable, while others seem quite
fanciful. All of this work is interesting, and some of it is quite
helpful in gaining a better understanding of the historical context
of the New Testament.[4]

Nevertheless, none of this scholarly work can alter the fact
that the four Gospels, as well as the other sections of the New
Testament that deal with Jesus, exist as historical testimony. Mark
may or may not have been written before Luke and Matthew. Luke
and Matthew may or may not have drawn on a common written
source other than Mark. Such claims are speculative and always
to some degree uncertain. In the end, even the most skeptical
scholars wind up taking at least *some* of that historical testimony
as credible. On the basis of their own theories they select from
what the New Testament and other ancient sources offer, and on

4. Recently, the work of the Jesus Seminar, a group of New Testament
scholars who take a very skeptical view of the Gospels, has received much
attention in the media. For a scholarly critique of their work, see Ben Withering-
ton III, *The Jesus Quest: The Third Search for the Jew of Nazareth* (Downers
Grove, IL: InterVarsity Press, 1995); Michael J. Wilkins and J. P. Moreland, *Jesus
under Fire: Modern Scholarship Reinvents the Historical Jesus* (Grand Rapids:
Zondervan Publishing House, 1995).

the basis of these speculative theories they decide which parts of the historical record are trustworthy. However, in light of the uncertain, speculative character of these theories, it would certainly appear reasonable at least to *consider* the historical record as a whole, not just those parts that fit with one's preconceived ideas about Jesus. It is certain that four authors, writing somewhere between twenty-five and sixty-five years after the events, have offered us testimony about Jesus of Nazareth. When someone offers us testimony, we must decide whether that testimony is credible.[5]

Why Believe Jesus Is God?

Why should a person believe the testimony of the New Testament? Granted that the New Testament views Jesus as God, why should someone accept it?

Christians have offered different kinds of answers to this question. Some have pointed to the authority of the church. If I believe the church is a reliable authority about such matters, and the church testifies that the New Testament is historically trustworthy, then it makes sense for me to accept this conclusion. Relying on authority is often the most reasonable stance for a layperson, and it is certainly not obvious that the church is necessarily less competent as an authority than skeptical academics who wish to use the authority of their scholarship to induce doubts. Nevertheless, an appeal to the authority of the church is likely to be unhelpful to many thoughtful people, because for them the question of the authority of the church is bound up with the question of the identity of Jesus. If Jesus is divine, then perhaps

5. For a defense of the historical reliability of the New Testament in light of the attacks of some skeptical historical scholars, see my *The Historical Christ and the Jesus of Faith: The Incarnational Narrative as History* (Oxford: Oxford University Press, 1996). In this work I argue that the historicity of the Gospel narratives is essential to Christian faith, and that contemporary historical scholarship does not undermine the reasonableness of faith in the truth of the narrative.

the church he founded is reliable, but they are not sure as to how to ascertain the authority of the church independently.

Another answer often given by Christians is that the truth of the New Testament is attested by God himself. There is a long theological tradition that the truth of the Bible is recognized through the "internal witness of the Holy Spirit." Many Christians claim that the Spirit of God does offer a kind of experiential support for the truth of the Bible in general and the New Testament in particular. They find that when they read the New Testament, they find themselves addressed by God. God speaks to them and reveals to them who they really are and who Jesus really is. They discover the answers to their deepest needs and fears.

Ultimately, I suspect that everyone who becomes a Christian will say that something like this is true. *After* a person has become a Christian, I suspect that he or she will come to understand that the whole process was guided by God. To be told this, however, may not be all that helpful to the person who is wondering whether to believe. Such a person needs a reason to believe the New Testament story is true. However, there is no reason the Spirit of God cannot work by helping a person to see this truth in a variety of ways, including helping a person to recognize that there are good reasons for such belief. The fact that Christian faith is ultimately the result of God at work within people does not mean that people who wonder about the truth of Christian faith cannot be given answers. So what sorts of reasons can be given?

Perhaps the best way to answer this question is to see why the earliest Christians believed in Jesus. What convinced them that Jesus was God?

Jesus' Claims about Himself

Certainly the background for their conviction was the knowledge of Jesus they had gained from his life, his teachings, and his whole ministry. Jesus' life is gripping. It was a life lived for others. He lived with the poor and downtrodden; he loved those whom everyone considered unlovable. He taught his followers to love their enemies and to forgive those who had wronged them. To his life and teachings must be added the many wonderful "signs" of Jesus — miracles of healing especially. Of course the early followers of Jesus were Jews, and their faith in him was also shaped by the conviction they had formed that Jesus had fulfilled God's promises in the Old Testament.

Against this background two things in particular stand out as evidence of Jesus' divinity. First and foremost were his own claims about himself. Jesus clearly used titles for himself that conveyed divinity. He called himself *Lord* and *Son of God*. He even used for himself the personal name of God, revealed by God to Moses, which was regarded by devout Jews as too sacred even to be pronounced. He forgave sins, not just sins against himself, but sins in which other people had been wronged, as if *he* had been the one offended. This makes sense only if all sin is regarded as an offense against God and if Jesus saw himself as God.

It is not easy to grasp how profoundly shocking these claims must have been to his contemporaries. The best way to understand this is simply to imagine someone you know today making similar claims. Imagine a neighbor who goes around preaching that you ought to repent, claiming to be God, and offering to forgive your sins. You would almost certainly regard him as insane. If you did not think him insane, you would certainly find him evil, a fraud who is probably out for power or money or both. The fact is you would find it impossible to be neutral about such a person. If you believed him, you would become a devoted follower. If you did not believe him, you would be repulsed.

This is precisely how people reacted to Jesus, and these reactions continue to be the only sensible ones. It makes no sense to regard such a man as a "simple moral teacher." Either he is who he claims to be or he is a lunatic or something worse than a lunatic. His contemporaries either became passionate followers or else were so repulsed they wanted to kill him. And the latter faction was clearly more numerous — and successful — at least in the short run.

But why wasn't everyone repulsed? Why did anyone accept such claims? Part of the answer clearly lies in Jesus' life. He was a profound teacher. To those who knew him intimately, he did not appear insane, and he certainly did not appear wicked. His words seemed to them to be clear, sober truth, not the ragings of a madman; and his ministry was shaped by self-giving love, not the lust after power, money, and fame that invariably accompanies the religious charlatan.

Jesus' Resurrection

Another significant reason why some people believed Jesus' claim is the second major piece of evidence that his claim was true. This is Jesus' resurrection. Jesus' resurrection was seen by his followers as a powerful confirmation of his claims, a divine guarantee that he was exactly who he claimed to be. For what better way could there be for God to vindicate the claims and message of a man who claimed to speak with divine authority than to raise that man from the dead?

But can one believe that Jesus really rose from the dead? Many people see this — and any miracle — as impossible. I will confront this perspective head-on in the next chapter. If you as a reader are convinced that miracles cannot occur, you may want to skip ahead to that chapter and then return. Or simply try to suspend judgment temporarily and keep an open mind on the question as to whether miracles occur.

For the fact is, there is impressive evidence of Jesus' resurrection for those who approach the evidence with an open mind.[6] At least three lines of evidence converge here.

First, there is the empty tomb itself. After Jesus' death, his tomb was sealed and guarded by Roman soldiers. It is hardly likely that Jesus' dispirited followers could or would have challenged such military might. Yet the body was gone from the tomb. If the body had not been gone, it would have been simple for the authorities to produce it and discredit Jesus' followers with their wild claim of a resurrection. The tradition of the empty tomb seems to have been accepted by all sides in the debate about Jesus that

6. For a powerful defense of the historical case for the resurrection, see Stephen Davis, *Risen Indeed: Making Sense of the Resurrection* (Grand Rapids: Wm. B. Eerdmans, 1993).

followed the witness of the apostles. Nor is it plausible to say, as some skeptics have maintained, that the location of Jesus' tomb was simply forgotten, since the burial place is identified as the tomb of Joseph of Arimathea, a prominent person whose tomb would have been publicly known.

Second, there is the testimony of those who saw the risen Jesus. Jesus appeared repeatedly to people. He appeared to individuals and he appeared to groups. He appeared to people who knew him intimately and to those who knew him only slightly. He appeared to people who were skeptical and those who were evidently surprised by the whole business.

It is particularly striking in this context that the earliest witnesses to Jesus' appearances were women. This makes it highly unlikely that these stories were invented by the early church. In the ancient world the testimony of women was regarded as worthless, and so if anyone were going to invent a story about Jesus appearing to credible witnesses, women would not have been good candidates for the job. Yet all the Gospels agree that the first witnesses were women, and all agree that the male disciples were initially unbelieving. This was an embarrassing story for the leadership of the early church, and therefore one that it would hardly have invented.

Finally, there is the impact of the resurrection on Jesus' followers. Jesus' disciples were transformed by his resurrection from a ragtag, dispirited group into a force of people who boldly challenged the world with their witness. They became people who were willing to suffer and to die for this claim. This fact is valuable partly because it lends weight to the second factor. If the resurrection did not occur and the witnesses made up the story, it is hard to see why they would be willing to suffer and die for such a concoction. Pascal puts the point bluntly: "I prefer those witnesses that get their throats cut."

But the transformation of the disciples is a fact that in its own right points to the resurrection. The disciples were willing to suffer beatings, stonings, and crucifixion because they were on fire with the knowledge that Jesus was Lord. His resurrection was a victory over sin and death in which his followers were invited to participate.

Jesus and the Individual

The arguments just given for Jesus' divinity seem to me to be strong ones. But it would be misleading to give the impression that Jesus' followers became his disciples merely by considering evidence or arguments. Nor do people become Christians that way today. Historical arguments in general are never absolutely compelling, and if this is true for historical evidence in general, it is doubly true for arguments that a single individual was God. It is surely for this reason that Christians maintain that faith in Jesus is ultimately the result of the work of the Spirit of God.

First of all, there is a gap between an intellectual recognition of who Jesus is and a commitment to him. Logically, it would seem that anyone who admits that Jesus is the Son of God should be willing to follow him and obey him. It is a truth that ought to transform their lives. But in fact there are many people who will give at least verbal assent to the proposition "Jesus is God," but who do not seem to care very much about Jesus, or even pay him much attention. It is clear then that what is necessary to become a Christian is not merely acceptance of a proposition on the basis of evidence, but *a change in a person's whole orientation to life.* Such changes are not produced solely by rational evidence of any kind, including historical evidence, because human beings are not solely rational creatures.

Second, even the evidence for Jesus' divinity has to be interpreted by each individual. We have already seen that if a person takes seriously the historical testimony of the New Testament about Jesus, it is reasonable to respond in one of two ways: either Jesus is God or he is a bad, perhaps insane, man. Jesus' disciples did not see him as bad or insane, yet there were those who saw him this way. How was this possible? The difference must lie in their own response to Jesus as a person. It is this encounter with Jesus that provides the context for the wildly different interpretations of the evidence.

By and large, then, faith is not simply a result of looking at intellectual facts. It is a result of encountering Jesus as a person. What makes the difference here? Who reacted badly to Jesus as a person?

It is clear enough from the New Testament that it was those people who were considered *good* who were most offended by Jesus, while those who responded in faith tended to be either notorious sinners or else very simple, unpretentious people. The reason for this is not hard to grasp. Jesus' message was a message that all have sinned; all are in need of repentance; all are in need of God. The movie star who believes she has it made, the big man on campus who believes he is really better than other people, the clever hypocrite who is good at seeing faults in others but misses her own failings — these are the ones who are farthest from the kingdom of God.

Perhaps we may find this reassuring. I may be tempted to say, "I'm no hypocrite like those pharisees, one of those self-righteous types." But such a smug feeling of superiority is already dangerously close to self-righteousness. The fact is, and contemporary psychologists have verified this, most of us do consider ourselves better than other people. We think we are more honest, more generous, and more conscientious than most everybody else. Jesus' message, then, is likely to offend almost everyone to some degree. It is hard for me to accept the fact that at bottom I have some genuinely nasty traits. It is hard to accept the fact that I am genuinely in need of God's help if I am to become like God and come to know God.

The crucial variable in how I respond to Jesus is ultimately how honest I am about my true condition and how much I desire to be helped. To people who come to Jesus with a willingness to admit their own inability to please God, or a willingness to learn this from Jesus, Jesus appears in a totally different light. To them Jesus is truly the divine suitor, the bringer of good news. For Jesus' life, death, and resurrection represent God's solution to *the* problem — the guilt, sin, and death that block me from that eternal life of love, which is my deepest desire.

On the other hand, people whose deepest thought about life is "I'm okay," who think they are doing pretty much what they should be doing and who feel no urgent need for a divine savior — such people are not likely to respond to Jesus' message with joy. To such people Jesus' message and Jesus' life are an insult and an intrusion. They are insults to their self-sufficiency and pretensions of righteousness, and intrusions on their desire to run their own lives.

The final challenge then to anyone who is seriously interested in Christianity is to go to the New Testament and meet the Jesus who is pictured there. Think about this Jesus, his life, his message, his death, and his resurrection. Think about your own failings and your own deepest needs and desires. Think as honestly as you can, and see if this Jesus creates in you a response of faith and trust as you get to know him. Perhaps you will discover that God has spoken to you.

CHAPTER NINE

Miracles and the Bible

Make no mistake: if He rose at all
it was His Body;
if the cells' dissolution did not reverse, the molecules
reknit, the amino acids rekindle,
the Church will fall. . . .
Let us not mock God with metaphor,
analogy, sidestepping, transcendence;
making of the event a parable, a sign painted in the
   faded
credulity of earlier ages:
let us walk through the door.

John Updike, *Seven Stanzas at Easter*

IT IS IMPOSSIBLE to use electrical light and the wireless and to avail ourselves of modern medical and surgical discoveries, and at the same time to believe in the New Testament world of spirits and miracles."[1] So said Rudolf Bultmann (1884–1976), an important European theologian.

There are three important things to notice in Bultmann's

---

1. Rudolf Bultmann, *Kerygma and Myth* (New York: Harper and Row, 1967), 5.

statement. First, he ties belief in "spirits and miracles" to belief in the New Testament. Such things are part of the New Testament's "world."

Second, it is evident that belief in "spirits and miracles" and in the New Testament has declined in the twentieth century. It has declined so much that even some who purport to be Christian theologians no longer can believe in them in the traditional way.

Third, Bultmann links the decline in belief in these things to the technology of Western civilization, which is in turn made possible by contemporary scientific discoveries.

I believe the chain of thought that underlies Bultmann's perspective goes something like this: (1) Modern science makes belief in miracles and spirits irrational. (2) We modern people commit ourselves to a scientific worldview when we embrace the technology that depends on that worldview. (3) Hence we cannot believe in spirits and miracles. (4) To the extent that the New Testament involves belief in spirits and miracles, then we cannot believe the New Testament. Bultmann is not alone in thinking this way.

Does God Act at the Retail Level?

This chain of thought raises two crucial issues. The first concerns the reliability and authority of the Bible. The second is the possibility and plausibility of miracles and spirits, or to speak more broadly, supernatural beings and events.

These two issues are connected in a number of ways. First, as already noted, the New Testament (and indeed the Bible as a whole) clearly teaches that miraculous events have occurred and that supernatural beings exist (angels, demons, and Satan, not to mention God himself).

Second, Christians have historically believed that the Bible itself is miraculous in its origin. Human beings wrote the Bible under inspiration by the Spirit of God, who worked through and did not override their normal human capacities, but nonetheless enabled them to produce something that natural human genius could not have accomplished on its own.

The underlying connection is simply this: Christians believe that the Bible and miracles involve "special acts of God." The Bible is a special revelation; miracles are events that reveal God's power and purposes in a special way. In believing in miracles and in special revelation Christianity is committed to a highly *personal* God.

Such a God does more than merely maintain the laws of nature. He does more than merely serve as the foundation for the moral law. He acts in special ways at special times. He calls Abram out of Ur and makes him Abraham, the father of many nations. He speaks to Moses in the burning bush and later gives him the Ten Commandments on Mount Sinai. He punishes Israel by giving the nation over to enemies, and he delivers the nation when the people turn back to him in repentance. In the New Testament he confronts Saul the persecutor on the road to Damascus and transforms him into Paul the apostle.

In short, the God of Christianity is highly individualized. To use a commercial metaphor, one might say he acts not merely at the wholesale level, but at the retail level as well. Such a God is highly embarrassing and irritating to many, precisely because he is so very personal.

It is all well and good to believe in a God who is thought of in vague terms as "a moral force," or "the power of being." Such a God will probably not interfere too much with my basic plans and values. He can for the most part be safely ignored. But the God of Christianity is a God who might *confront* me. He is a God who might ask me to give some (or all) of my money to the poor, to sacrifice my own pleasures for others. He is a God who threatens my autonomy, my desire to make *myself* God. He is also a threat to the false gods I have erected, gods such as nationalism, materialism, and ambition. He can't be ignored; he is *aware* of me. I can no more ignore his presence than I could ignore the presence of a stranger in a small elevator.

The issue as to whether God acts in special ways is therefore a crucial one for anyone who is a follower of Jesus or who is considering becoming a follower. I will deal first with the reliability and authority of the Bible, viewed as a special revelation. This will lead to a consideration of the reasonableness of belief in miracles.

With a proper understanding of miracles, I will then return to the issue of biblical authority.

Jesus and the Authority of the Bible

The Bible is fundamental to Christian faith. It is God's word to us, as the Westminster Confession puts it, "given by inspiration of God, to be the rule of faith and life." Why do Christians believe that?

The fundamental reason lies in the authority of Jesus. If a person accepts Jesus' bold claim to be the Son of God, a claim that must be blasphemous if it is not true, then he or she ought to accept Jesus' teachings as truthful. From all that can be known of Jesus, it is clear that he accepted the Old Testament as the word of God, a fully truthful and reliable expression of God to humans.[2] The New Testament was written by the apostles, those people whom Jesus selected to carry on his work and to whom he gave a special authority, or by people who were very closely associated with Jesus' apostles. A person who accepts Jesus' authority will naturally accept the authority of those whom Jesus selected to carry on his work.[3]

It might appear that this is a circular enterprise. The authority of the Bible is accepted on the basis of the authority of Jesus. But Jesus is only really known to us through the Bible. So aren't we really starting by assuming what we want to conclude, that the Bible is reliable?

There is no real circularity in this reasoning. It is true that Christians begin with a confrontation with Jesus as presented in the Bible. But they do *not* begin by assuming the Bible is inspired by God. In our argument for Jesus' divinity in the last chapter, we were very

2. Jesus' recorded teachings contain hundreds of quotations and allusions to the Old Testament, and Jesus constantly uses the Old Testament as an authority. See Luke 24:25-27, 44-45 and Matthew 5:17-18 for especially clear examples of Jesus' view of the Old Testament.

3. Later in this chapter I briefly discuss what it might mean to affirm the full truthfulness of the Bible. See pp. 91-93.

careful to begin with the Bible as an ordinary historical document, with no assumptions about its being infallible or divinely inspired.

The point is simply this. Regardless of whether the Bible is inspired or possesses any special authority, it undeniably *exists* as a historical document. It contains the testimony of people who claimed to have seen and heard Jesus, and the testimony of people who knew intimately those who claimed to have had such experiences. As testimony, it confronts the reader with Jesus and asks the reader to make a decision about him.

Christians are people who respond to this encounter with faith. Because of their faith in the Jesus they have discovered, they will also accept Jesus' teachings about the Bible. Although the Bible is extremely important to Christians, we must not lose sight of the important truth that the basis of Christianity is faith in Jesus. Faith in the Bible as the word of God depends on faith in Jesus, and not vice versa. The argument for biblical authority from Jesus' authority is not circular.

Still, it is true that unbelievers must at least be willing to view the Bible as a historical witness if they are to become believers. They must regard it as a piece of testimony that could conceivably be true, even though they do not have to regard it as God's word. Many people find it very difficult to do this. One important barrier to acceptance of the Bible as a historical record is the many miracle stories that it contains. Skeptics about the Bible think, like Bultmann, that miracles just can't happen and therefore that a book that contains many accounts of such things cannot be historically reliable. It is crucial, then, to examine this conviction that miracles are impossible.

Are Miracles Possible?

Why do many people believe that miracles are impossible? Often the reasons are not very good ones. One reason may simply be that a person has been told that "modern educated people" don't believe in such things, or even, with Bultmann, that such people *cannot* believe in such things.

Now it is obviously true that many people do find it difficult or even impossible to believe in miracles today. Just as obviously, however, many educated people can and do believe in miracles. (Sometimes people in one group may be so culturally isolated that they don't know anyone in the other group.) It's hard to see how such psychological or sociological facts cut much ice either way. For while it is true that what people find believable sometimes may reflect rational evidence, just as often it reflects peculiarities in upbringing or even the intellectual fads of an era. (There was a time when most people found it impossible to believe that the world is round.) If enough people believe that miracles are impossible, they may well succeed in making belief in miracles a "dead option" for many people *even if their conviction is baseless.*

If we want seriously and honestly to grapple with the question as to whether miracles are possible, we are better off simply forgetting about "modern people," and what they can or cannot believe. Instead, we ought to focus on the question of what we *should* believe. We simply ought to recognize that if we affirm that we cannot believe in miracles, it might show our intellectual depth, but it might also be a confession of a personal failing, such as an impoverished imagination.

Many people reject the possibility of miracles because they don't believe in God. This certainly is more reasonable than the kind of sociological view that claims belief in miracles is outdated. Of course, if there is no God, there are no special acts of God. But if I reject miracles because I reject God, you should ask me how I really *know* there is no God. After all, *not knowing there is a God* is not the same as *knowing there is no God.* And if it is possible for God to exist, then I cannot claim to know that miracles are impossible on *that* basis.

It is true that our estimate of the likelihood of a miracle is strongly influenced by our view of the likelihood of God's existence. This is one reason why the clues for God's reality, the calling cards discussed in Chapters Four through Six, are so significant. From a Christian perspective, it is not that this "natural" knowledge of God is so important in itself. Certainly we cannot gain from these clues the kind of knowledge of God that we were meant to possess. Rather, these clues are ways of getting our attention, alerting us to the fact that there is someone behind and above the natural world.

From the mere fact that God exists, one cannot deduce that miracles will happen. But if God is real and if he is the sort of intelligent being suggested by the design in the universe, then miracles seem at least possible. And if God has planted within us a desire to know him and a need to experience him (as was argued in Chapter Six), then this suggests he is a personal being who has a genuine concern for us. Perhaps he would seek to communicate with us in a special way so as to give us a real knowledge of himself. Perhaps he might want to signal the importance of his message by other "special acts."

Another reason for believing that miracles are impossible may be the most common one of all, even though it's not a very good one. Many people find it hard to believe in miracles simply because they have never experienced one. It is human nature to be comfortable with what is familiar and to distrust what is unfamiliar. It is very natural and common to generalize from our own limited experience. Since few people have experienced miracles, it is understandable that it is hard for most of us to accept their possibility.

A moment's reflection, however, shows how weak this is as a reason to deny the possibility of miracles. Genuine miracles will almost certainly be rare and unusual events. Things that happen every day to everybody are by definition not miracles. For me to conclude that miracles are impossible because I have not experienced one is both foolish and arrogant.

Miracles and Science

Probably the strongest argument against miracles derives from the authority of science. Many people claim that miracles cannot occur because they would violate the laws of nature discovered by science.

To deal with this problem we must first carefully think about the definition of a miracle. Miracles are usually thought of as events that cannot be given a natural explanation but must be attributed directly to God, who has acted in a special way in the natural order. Thus a miracle is an "interruption" in the natural order.

Not all Christians are happy with this conception of a miracle. They rightly emphasize the fact that God is responsible for all natural processes. Therefore an event that can be given a natural explanation can also be regarded as the work of God. So sometimes miracles are defined as astounding events that, because of their rarity or because of the time and place they occur, serve as a special sign of God's power and character, even if they have a natural explanation.

Thus, if the parting of the Red Sea for the children of Israel was due to a strong east wind and if the wind can be explained as an ordinary meteorological phenomenon, this does not prevent it from being a miracle on this definition. God is responsible for all natural processes, and the timing of this unusual event suggests God's providential care for Israel. If this view of miracles is correct, then there is obviously no conflict between belief in miracles and belief in scientific laws, since miracles don't involve any exceptions to or "breaks" from those laws.

It must be admitted, however, that many of the miracles in the Bible do appear to involve what are sometimes misleadingly called "breaks" or "interruptions" in the natural order. It is very difficult to see how a natural, scientific explanation could be given of a man's walking on water or of someone coming back to life after being dead for three days. And many Christians do believe that miracles of this type involve a special action of God in the natural order.

It is, however, somewhat incorrect to call such special actions "breaks" or "interruptions" in the natural order. Such terminology implies that God is not normally present in the natural order; but if God exists at all, then he must be regarded as responsible for the whole of that natural order. The contrast, then, is not between "nature" and very unusual divine "interventions" into nature, but between God's normal activity in upholding the natural order and some special activity on God's part. Thus, when God does a miracle, he does not suddenly enter a created order from which he is normally absent. Rather, he acts in a special way in a natural order which he continually upholds and in which he is constantly present.

Suppose it is true that at least some miracles are events that cannot be explained scientifically because they seem to go against well-known laws of nature. Would such miracles be "violations" of laws of nature? Could such events occur?

To answer these questions we must ask another: What is a law of nature? Or, to be more precise, If there is a God, what are laws of nature? In this context it is perfectly legitimate to think on the assumption that God exists. If God does *not* exist, then it is obvious that miracles cannot occur. So anyone who is seriously interested in the possibility of miracles must be willing to admit the *possibility* of God's existence.

The question "What is a law of nature?" is a difficult one. Some philosophers of science believe that natural laws are purely descriptive. They simply describe the orderly way in which nature behaves. Other philosophers believe that laws of nature do not merely tell us what in fact happens, but what in some sense *must* happen. It is not that the laws themselves make anything occur, but they reflect underlying necessities in the structure of nature.

From the Christian viewpoint, neither of these two views is any threat to the possibility of miracles. If God exists, and the laws of nature are purely descriptive, then those laws simply describe God's normal actions as he maintains the universe in an orderly way. The fact that God normally works in a certain way hardly shows that it is impossible for him to act differently on a special occasion for some special purpose.

If the laws of nature are viewed as more than just descriptive of what in fact happens, then the case is a little more complicated. However, this way of looking at laws of nature is also compatible with miracles. If God exists, then any "necessary" features of the natural order reflect his will in creation. If matter must behave in a certain way, it is because God has willed a particular structure to exist that results in a particular pattern. But if this pattern ultimately depends on God's will, there does not seem to be any reason why God could not will an exception to the pattern. Of course that would mean that the "necessary" patterns of the natural order are not *absolutely* necessary, just necessary relative to God's will. They describe what *must* happen unless God wills otherwise. But if God exists (and unless he does, miracles are impossible anyway), then no feature of nature can exist absolutely independent of his will. It seems therefore that God could indeed cause an event that would be an exception to the laws of nature.

If God were to act in such a special way, the action would not accurately be described as a *violation* of a law. If there is a God, the laws of nature are not rules to which God must submit, but the expression of his will. If he wills something different on a particular occasion, then an exceptional event occurs, but there is nothing analogous to a human being breaking or violating a law.

A Religious Objection to Miracles

Some still feel that such an act would be unworthy of God in some sense. Perhaps they have a vague sense that such an action would be inconsistent on God's part, a sign that he had failed in some way. Certainly Christians would agree that God must be consistent; his basic character and intentions do not change. The question is whether this means that God must order nature with rigid laws from which no deviations are ever permitted.

It is easy to see why God might want to create a natural order with a dependable structure. Such an orderly nature makes it possible for humans to anticipate the consequences of their actions. It also makes it possible for God to "withdraw" somewhat so that his presence in nature is not so obvious that humans who do not care to know him are forced to acknowledge him, as discussed in Chapter One. However, I see no reason why the order in nature would have to be absolutely rigid.

Reasonable people often do have set patterns to which they generally conform. But a person who cannot deviate from a set pattern for a special occasion or in special circumstances is more aptly described as obsessive than as rational. Nor is special behavior in special circumstances a sign of inconsistency. Rather, truly creative people show a deeper consistency — to their ultimate values and purposes — by responding creatively to a unique situation.

A man who lives in downtown Manhattan may normally walk to work. On a special day he may have good reasons for taking a cab, but this exception to his usual procedure is hardly a sign that he is inconsistent or irresponsible.

If Jesus is God in human form, God's action to save a fallen humanity, then this is clearly a unique event. It is hardly surprising that Jesus' life would be accompanied by miracles as a sign of the power of God that was focused in him. Nor is it surprising that God's redemptive activity in the life of Israel that led up to Jesus' life should occasionally show the same special power, or that the life of the church that Jesus established should also at times reveal God at work in special ways.

The Bible as Special Revelation

If miracles are possible, then the fact that the Bible contains miracles is no barrier to its being historically accurate. For the New Testament particularly, the many ancient and reliable copies of the text in existence and the fact that the books were written quite close in time to the events recounted mean that it must be taken seriously as historical testimony. It is up to each of us to decide what to make of the Jesus who is described there, the Jesus who demands a hearing by the awesome claims he makes and the many well-attested miracles that back up those claims, especially his resurrection. As we saw earlier in this chapter, it is quite reasonable for the person who responds to Jesus in faith also to accept the Bible as a special revelation from God. The accounts of miracles that the Bible contains, far from being a barrier to its acceptance, are a sign that God was at work in the events recounted.

Many people of course take a very critical view of the Bible, insisting that the various books were written much later than the events reported and that the Bible contains a great deal of accumulated myths and legends.[4] We cannot go deeply into this con-

4. For a clear review of the evidence for early dating of the New Testament and for its general historical reliability, see F. F. Bruce, *The New Testament Documents: Are They Reliable?* rev. ed. (Downers Grove, IL: InterVarsity Press, 1960).

troversy, and it is important to remember that the Christian's faith in Jesus is what is foundational, not faith in any particular theory of biblical inspiration.[5] However, it is worth pointing out that many of the "critical" views of the Bible are not solidly rooted in purely historical or textual evidence. Rather, they reflect philosophical assumptions on the part of the critics.[6]

Because a passage from the Bible contains a seemingly accurate prophecy, the critic assumes the passage must have been written later than the events that fulfilled the prophecy. The conclusion is not based on textual evidence primarily, but on the prior assumption that miraculous prophecies cannot occur.

Or a passage that contains an account of a miracle is assumed to be a later addition by a pious follower. Again, the reason may be a prior assumption that miracles cannot happen, not independent textual evidence.

It should be obvious that such critical theories are rooted more in a philosophical suspicion of special acts of God than they are in objective evidence. And when we look at these philosophical suspicions with a critical eye, there is little basis for them, as we have seen, regardless of how widespread and popular they may be, and regardless of how many would-be sociologists (or confused theologians) tell us that modern people cannot believe in miracles. If miracles are possible, there is no reason why God could not inspire human authors to communicate a message from him and guide their authorship in such a manner that the message is communicated in a truthful and reliable manner.

Christians who accept the authority of the Bible on the basis

5. For a classical account of this kind of case for the historic Christian view of the Bible, see B. B. Warfield, *The Inspiration and Authority of the Bible* (Philadelphia: Presbyterian and Reformed, 1948), esp. "The Real Problem of Inspiration," 160-226. For a very brief account of the arguments on both sides that highlights the role of philosophical assumptions, see Richard Purtill, "The Bible: Myth or History," in *Thinking about Religion* (Englewood Cliffs, NJ: Prentice-Hall, 1978).

6. See chapter 14 of my *The Historical Christ and the Jesus of Faith: The Incarnational Narrative as History* (Oxford: Oxford University Press, 1966), for some concrete examples of dubious literary and philosophical assumptions on the part of some of the more skeptical biblical scholars.

of their faith in Jesus accept various theories of biblical inspiration. Almost all agree that inspiration is not a mechanical process of dictation. God used the ordinary capacities of the human authors, and many would say that in some cases this involved the human author's using an oral tradition or some written sources. But they would insist that God was providentially working through the process and guiding it.

Some Christians believe that God's inspiration means that the Bible is completely truthful on everything it touches, including historical details and even scientific facts. (Though even those who affirm such a completely "inerrant" Bible will recognize that what counts as a "mistake" must take into account the standards of accuracy of the day and the intentions of the author; everyone recognizes such points as the use of round numbers, and the arrangement of teachings ascribed to Jesus in the gospels by theme rather than in strict chronological order.)[7]

Others say that inspiration only means that the Bible is truthful and reliable about those matters God intended to teach us about: mainly basic truths about God and the human condition, the history of God's redemptive actions, and teachings about how to respond to God and live a new life. All agree that the Bible is essential to the Christian's faith. The Bible is a revelation from God to us. If it did not exist, we would be limited to those general clues to himself God has planted in nature and human experience. It is not surprising, therefore, that Christians accord to the Bible a special authority in trying to understand the implications of their new life in Christ. This is especially true for those who agree that an acceptance of Jesus' authority ought to lead to accepting the Bible as more than an ordinary historical document. For them the Bible is the inspired word of God.

Of course inspiring human authors to write a book would be a rather "special" special act of God, in part because such an action is difficult to detect. How could it be known that an author was

7. For a helpful discussion of what it does and does not mean to affirm the full truthfulness of the Bible, see "The Words of Jesus in the Gospels: Live, Jive, or Memorex?" in *Jesus under Fire,* ed. Michael J. Wilkins and J. P. Moreland (Grand Rapids: Zondervan Publishing House, 1995), 73-100.

more than just truthful or profound, that he in fact had a special message from God? One way might be for God to give a "signal" or sign that something important is going on by doing more obvious miracles. The miracles performed by the prophets, the apostles, and Jesus, far from being a barrier to belief in the Bible, are therefore just what one would expect if the Bible is a true revelation from God. They are miracles that authenticate the miracle of the Bible itself.

This has been a long and somewhat difficult chapter, so let me try to summarize my conclusions:

1. Miracles as special acts of God are possible, and it is possible to have good evidence for miracles.
2. Therefore, the fact that the Bible contains accounts of miracles is no reason to think it is unreliable.
3. One kind of miracle that God is capable of is that of revealing himself by giving special inspiration to humans.
4. Jesus accepted the Bible as authoritative, and those who accept Jesus' authority ought therefore to accept the Bible's authority as well.
5. The miracle accounts contained in the Bible of the wonders performed by the prophets, the apostles, and Jesus himself are signs that certify that God was at work revealing himself, and therefore that the Bible is the word of God.

CHAPTER TEN

Why Would a Good God Allow . . . ?

> Epicurus's old questions are yet unanswered. Is he [God]
> willing to prevent evil, but not able? then he is impotent.
> Is he able but not willing? then he is malevolent. Is he
> both able and willing? whence then is evil?
>
> Philo in David Hume,
Dialogues Concerning Natural Religion

MOST OF US find it difficult to comprehend cruelty; we find it
hard to believe that such things as rapes, torture and murders
could happen. Yet it is clear from history's sordid tale that cruelty
has been a regular occurrence, and, as the evening news only too
regularly reveals, it still is. Ivan, in *The Brothers Karamazov*,
meditates on this aspect of human existence:

> "By the way, a Bulgarian I met lately in Moscow," Ivan went
> on, seeming not to hear his brother's words, "told me about the
> crimes committed by Turks and Circassians in all parts of
> Bulgaria through fear of a general rising of the Slavs. They burn
> villages, murder, outrage women and children, they nail their
> prisoners by the ears to the fences, leave them so till morning,
> and in the morning they hang them — all sorts of things you

can't imagine. People talk sometimes of bestial cruelty, but that's a great injustice and insult to the beasts; a beast can never be so cruel as a man, so artistically cruel. The tiger only tears and gnaws, that's all he can do. He would never think of nailing people by the ears, even if he were able to do it. These Turks took a pleasure in torturing children, too; cutting the unborn child from the mother's womb, and tossing babies up in the air and catching them on the points of their bayonets before their mother's eyes. Doing it before the mother's eyes was what gave zest to the amusement. Here is another scene I thought very interesting. Imagine a trembling mother with her baby in her arms, a circle of invading Turks around her. They've planned a diversion; they pet the baby, laugh to make it laugh. They succeed, the baby laughs. At that moment a Turk points a pistol four inches from the baby's face. The baby laughs with glee, holds out its little hands to the pistol, and he pulls the trigger in the baby's face and blows out its brains. Artistic, wasn't it? By the way, Turks are particularly fond of sweet things, they say."

Ivan's speech is a wrenching experience. The suffering caused by such horrible actions is hard to imagine, but it is none the less real. We cannot comfort ourselves by thinking that such incidents happened only in the past when human beings were less "civilized." Each decade seems to offer new horrors: the Cambodia of a Pol Pot or the "ethnic cleansing" of a Bosnia. When we add to this evil the suffering caused by natural disasters, tragic accidents, and the ordinary diseases that wrench apart families every day, it is easy to see why life has so often been called "a vale of tears." All of this suffering creates a genuine difficulty for Christian faith. Why does God permit such things? Why has he made a world where so many, including innocent children, suffer so much?

These questions can be asked in many different voices, with many different concerns. They are asked by believers, courageously hanging on to their faith that there is an answer, longing to know what it might be, while painfully aware of their ignorance. These questions are also asked by honest searchers, wanting to believe but fearing that faith may require them to hide from unpleasant truths. They are asked by hostile skeptics, confident that faith can be shown to be illogical and morally questionable. We will try to pose the issues from each of these standpoints.

Can God's Existence Be Disproved?

When posed by the atheist or the hostile agnostic, the question about suffering is not really a question at all, but an assertion. Many antireligious thinkers have claimed that the existence of evil *proves* that the kind of God Christians believe in does not exist. Or at least they claim that evil provides strong evidence against God's existence.

The argument here is simple and ancient. God is supposed to be both completely powerful and completely good. A totally good being, one who was all-loving, would prevent suffering whenever possible. A completely powerful being would be able to prevent all suffering and evil. Therefore, if God exists, there should be no suffering. But there is plenty of suffering. Therefore, either God does not exist, or else he is not both completely powerful and fully good. From this standpoint evil is very powerful evidence against the reality of the God of the Bible (or any God who is, like the God of the Bible, both completely good and all-powerful).

To answer this attack we must think more deeply about God's nature. The Christian will certainly agree that God must be seen as all-powerful and as completely good, thoroughly just and loving. But is it true that an all-powerful being can prevent all evil? And would a completely good God want to prevent all suffering?

Let us take the latter question first. There are many cases in which a good earthly parent could prevent suffering yet chooses not to do so. Some cases are obvious. A parent could prevent any chance that a child would be hurt in an automobile accident by never allowing the child to leave the house. Such a course of action would certainly prevent a good deal of suffering — auto accidents are a leading cause of death and injuries to children — but no reasonable parent would opt for such a policy.

A more realistic example might be a parent of a teenager who allows the young person some choice as to whom his or her friends and associates will be. The parent could probably spare the young person some mistakes (and suffering) by making all such choices for the teenager. However, a good parent elects not to do that, reasoning that at least within limits the young person ought to have this freedom, and indeed must have it if he or she is to become a mature adult.

The point of these examples is that an assumption that seems to be required for the antireligious argument is mistaken. The assumption is that a good person always eliminates all the suffering it is possible to prevent. The truth is that there are times when a good person will allow suffering for the sake of some higher good. Parents, for example, do not want their children to suffer, and they do try to prevent such suffering. But they also do not want their children to remain infantile in their personalities, and they realize that the goal of growth may sometimes require that they allow their children to make their own mistakes and suffer accordingly.

Good persons do not necessarily eliminate all the suffering they can, then. Rather, they prevent suffering where it is possible to do so without harming some more important goal. Christians believe that God acts in a way similar to parents. He cares about suffering, but frequently permits it for the sake of other, higher goals. (What these might be will be discussed presently.)

At this point the antireligious argument points to the other crucial truth about God, that he is supposed to be all-powerful. Perhaps human parents, being finite, must allow suffering in order to achieve other goals. Surely God, who is all-powerful, ought to be able to achieve all his goals without suffering.

To answer this charge we must think more about an all-powerful being. Can God do literally anything? Could he make a square circle, for instance, or a person who was not a person? Most Christians agree that the answer to these questions must be no. A square circle is not a real possibility at all; it is not a possible object that could or could not be made. A person who is not a person is nothing at all. God could not create such things, but this is no real limitation on God's power, for the simple reason that these things are not really possible "things" at all.

So there are in fact some "limits" even to what an all-powerful being can do. Some of these limitations are relevant to the question as to whether God could achieve his purposes without allowing any suffering. Suppose, for instance, that one of God's purposes is to create free beings who would love and serve him by their own choice. It's easy to see that such love is an important good, one that might justify some risk of suffering. Love that is compelled or forced is not genuine love, and yet almost everyone recognizes the value of love. This is the kind of insight that underlies wise parents who gradually give their children freedom. Of course this freedom may be misused, and thus giving it is risky. But it is exactly this sort of freedom that makes a human person a person and not a robot. Parents would surely prefer the "risky" love of a genuine human being to the "sure thing" of a clever humanlike robot who is programmed to "love" them.

But couldn't God create free beings who would always freely love him? Perhaps God could create free beings who always do in fact freely love and serve him. Perhaps he has, on other planets, or among the angels. However, God could not create free beings and *guarantee* that they would always use their freedom wisely. Inherent in the idea that a human person is free to perform an act is that the person be free not to perform the act. A human person who is free and yet cannot choose wrongly is a person who is both free and not free. Not even God could create such a "round square."

Christians have traditionally affirmed that at least a great deal of suffering in the world is due to God's granting freedom to us. Murders, thefts, rapes, the miseries of war, are all traceable to our decisions. Even the devastation of famine could be avoided if we were willing to share what we have with those less fortunate, for enough food is produced on this planet to feed everyone.

Can We Justify God's Ways?

At this point two objections are apt to occur. First, we may think that freedom isn't really worth it. The amount of suffering shows that God paid too high a price, one a truly good being would not have been willing to pay. Second, we may think that a lot of suffering does not seem to be related to human choices at all, the suffering that stems from diseases and from natural disasters such as earthquakes and tornadoes, for example.

Some Christians have tried to directly counter both of these objections. They have argued that the value of freedom clearly outweighs the suffering in this life when we consider the fact that this life is only a speck in comparison with the eternal life that awaits us after death. In eternity God will surely compensate those who have suffered unjustly and even help them to use their sufferings to become the kinds of persons they could not otherwise be. And they have countered the second claim by arguing that diseases and disasters may be connected to the free choices of fallen angels or other supernatural beings, or may be in some mysterious way a consequence of human sin, the result of a divine judgment on the earth as the habitat of a fallen race.

Such arguments are attempts to prove that freedom is really worth it and to explain just why God allows evil and suffering. But should Christians be able to prove that God was justified in creating free beings? Ought Christians to be able to explain why God allows suffering in all cases? Perhaps many Christians would like to be able to do these things, but on deeper reflection we can see that there is no real reason why Christians should be able to give such explanations. In reality, it would be surprising if they were able to know such things.

Let us look at the situation again. We are looking at the problem of evil as a challenge posed by the atheist or hostile agnostic, the person who thinks that suffering provides powerful evidence against the existence of God. The initial challenge to belief was a claim that an all-powerful, all-loving God would not permit any suffering, because a good being always prevents all the suffering it can. We have seen that this claim is unfounded, because there clearly are situations where a good being will allow some suffering in order to achieve a higher goal and because there are some goods — freely given love, for example — which not even God could achieve without allowing the possibility of suffering.

At this point someone may wonder whether freedom is really worth it, and also what God's reasons for allowing other kinds of suffering might be. And well he or she might wonder, for these are difficult questions. To answer them, what kind of knowledge would we have to possess? Really, we would have to have exhaustive knowledge of God's purposes in creation and of his plans for eternity. Only then could we *know* that freedom is not worth the cost or *know* that God had no good reason for allowing natural diseases, and so on. Clearly we human beings do not and cannot have this knowledge.

This limitation is not surprising to the Christian, nor is it really disturbing. Human beings are finite creatures and should not expect fully to understand God, who is the infinite Creator.

However, this limitation *is* disturbing to the skeptic, whose claim is that evil proves that God does not exist. It is now clear that no one can actually know this unless her or his own knowledge is godlike. The skeptic's challenge is really presumptuous and arrogant. It is a claim by a finite creature to know how the world should have been created. How could a skeptic know such a thing? Evil is not a disproof of God's existence. There may be questions about evil that we cannot answer, but our ignorance is far from a conclusive argument against God's reality. Instead, it means we humans are not in a position to mount such an argument.

Does Evil Make Faith in God Unreasonable?

We noted at the beginning of this chapter that the question about evil can be asked from various perspectives. The first perspective we have examined is one in which the question is not really posed as a question at all, but as a hostile challenge to faith. We have seen that this challenge fails; evil is not decisive evidence against God's reality.

We must remember, however, that the questions about evil can also be asked in a different spirit. A sincere seeker who would like to believe in a good God but wonders whether such faith is reasonable asks such questions too. Our response to this challenge in the last section may make this difficulty appear even more severe. If we are not in a position clearly and decisively to know God's reasons for allowing evil, then can we be confident that a good God exists? Even if the atheist cannot prove that God has no good reason for allowing evil, do Christians have any reason for believing he does?

They certainly do. Christians can very well have solid reasons for believing that God has reasons for allowing evil, even if they do not know what these reasons are. (That doesn't mean that Christians never do know what God's reasons are for allowing evil.) It's perfectly possible to have strong evidence that someone has a good reason for an action without knowing what that reason might be.

An example might help here. Thinking back a few years to when my children were still small, let us suppose my wife, Jan, has gone out for an evening to do some shopping, leaving me to take care of the children. She knows that I have some important work to do, and assures me she will be home by nine. Ten P.M. arrives and Jan is still not home. The baby (who is still being breast-fed) is hungry and irritable, and I am beginning to match his disposition.

What is her reason for staying out an hour later than she promised? I really have no idea. Abstractly considered, there are many possibilities. Perhaps she bumped into an old friend, who just had to talk. Possibly she has had an accident, or the car broke down. Maybe she decided to go dancing at a singles bar.

I have no way of knowing what her actual reason is. Nevertheless, I have strong evidence that she has a reason and that her reason is a good one. If I am thinking clearly and coolly in the face of the baby's distress (which is not always easy), I will not be angry or irritable at her. For she surely would not be so late unless she had a good reason.

What is my evidence for that, when I have no idea what her reason is? My evidence, to put it simply, is all the knowledge I already have of my wife. I know the kind of person she is. I know she is not the kind of person to go dancing at a singles bar and leave me alone with the children. She loves me, she cares about me, and she lives up to her commitments. Therefore, if she is later than she promised, she has a good reason.

Christians believe that their relation to God is very much like this. If God permits evil, then he must have a good reason, even if we don't know what that reason is. Our evidence for this is simply our total knowledge of God's character. God loves us, God cares about us, and God honors his commitments.

But how do we gain this knowledge of God's character? To some degree a knowledge of God's goodness may stem from the "clues" that God has planted in our experience, particularly our moral experience. However, Christians would agree with unbelievers here that if we had to go only on our natural knowledge, then our belief in God's goodness would be quite shaky. No, the fundamental source of our knowledge of God's character is God's self-revelation in the Bible, especially in Jesus.

If we believe that Jesus is God's supreme revelation, then we can hardly help but see God's character as totally loving and just. It is not just Jesus' teaching that is at issue here, though that is significant. It is Jesus' life, death, and resurrection. For Jesus is God in human form, a God who not only tells us he cares about our sufferings, but *shows* us he cares. He shows us by living with us in poverty, manifesting love to the sick and the poor. Ultimately, he shows us by suffering with us an ignominious and painful death. Then, by the power of God, Jesus' resurrection is a promise that God can bring meaning out of suffering, that he can and will turn defeat into victory. Death and sin will be vanquished.

The implication of this for those who wonder whether God has a reason for allowing evil is clear. They do not need a philosophical argument. Rather they need to get to know God and understand his character. They need to be pointed to Jesus.

But What about Doubts?

Suppose we do discover God in the person of Jesus. Does that mean we will cease to wonder about evil and suffering? Is it possible for believers to struggle with the question of God's goodness?

Not only is it possible, it happens all the time. Christians suffer, just as do non-Christians. And they not only suffer themselves, they hurt with other victims. Such feelings often lead Christians to wonder why God allows things to happen the way they do. Such wondering is often more than intellectual; it is an anguished bafflement.

These feelings and questions are honest and real. I myself do not think they are sinful. Though they may be the occasion for sin, God knows our humanness and our ignorance. He *wants* us to care about suffering. He *wants* us to be outraged at the way things go on. The Psalms in the Bible often reflect such outrage. God does *not* want us glibly to explain away suffering with proofs that this is "the best of all possible worlds." For the world we live in is a fallen world, a world that does not function as it was intended to function.

Christians also ask "why?" in the face of suffering and evil. But they ask not in the spirit of a presumptuous challenge but as God's children. They ask as earthly children might inquire of an earthly father whose actions are sometimes hard to understand. If the relationship is a tender and healthy one, those earthly children will not be afraid to ask their questions, and they can be confident the father will not be angry with them for asking. But they will also know that sometimes the answers may not be forthcoming, and in that case they must trust in their father's wisdom.

Those of us who raise questions about God's goodness do not usually need philosophical arguments, nor do we need spiritual rebuke. We need new assurance of God's love, new experience of his character. One way that can happen is for us to experience God's love in the love and support of other people.

Christian philosophers have given strong refutations of the claims of atheists to have disproved God's existence on the basis of evil. However, the best answers Christians can ultimately give to the problem of evil are two. First, they can point to Jesus, who reveals God's goodness and love and suffers with us. Second, they can follow Jesus' example by working against suffering, and suffering with those who suffer.

CHAPTER ELEVEN

But Isn't Religion Just . . . ?

We understand how a primitive man is in need of a god as creator of the universe, as chief of his clan, as personal protector. . . . A man of later days, of our own day, behaves in the same way. He, too, remains childish and in need of protection, even when he is grown up; he thinks he cannot do without support from his god.

Sigmund Freud, *Moses and Monotheism*

The criticism of religion disillusions man so that he will think, act and fashion his reality as a man who has lost his illusions and regained his reason; so that he will revolve about himself as his own true sun. Religion is only the illusory sun about which man revolves so long as he does not revolve about himself.

Karl Marx, "Contribution to the Critique of Hegel's *Philosophy of Right:* Introduction"

THIS BOOK BEGAN with the story of Jim losing his faith in college. Part of Jim's problem was that he had no positive reason to believe that Christianity was actually true. We have attempted to supply this lack for someone in Jim's situation in Chapters Three through

Eight. However, Jim's problem was not simply that he lacked positive reasons to think Christianity was true. He also had (or thought he had) strong reasons for *not* believing, for viewing Christianity as false.

One of these reasons, perhaps the weightiest, is the problem of suffering, which was addressed in the previous chapter. There are, however, many other skeptical challenges. A year on a typical university campus would expose most people to the charge that Christian belief is unscientific, that it is a psychological "projection," that it is sexist and oppressive of women, and generally a tool of reactionary political and economic perspectives. Obviously each of these challenges raises a host of issues, but I will briefly try to explain each challenge and some possible responses.

Is Christianity Unscientific?

Our first challenge comes dressed in the clothes of science. Christianity, like other religions, is seen as a prescientific, mythological view of things. Christian belief arose in the days when everyone thought that the earth was the center of the universe. The early Christians taught that the sky above the earth contained a literal heaven, while below the earth was a literal hell. Even today Christians are stuck with beliefs that clearly violate scientific knowledge: that the earth was created very recently and that all humans are descended from a historical Adam and Eve, for example.

Such beliefs were understandable and forgivable before the age of scientific knowledge, says the skeptic. It was, after all, common in ancient times to explain what humans did not understand as the result of the gods' work. Today, however, the universe can be explained as a result of matter behaving in accordance with scientific laws.

It is really unjust to science to call this skeptic a "scientist," for genuine science actually gives these claims no support. Few great scientists have had such a superficial view of either science or Christian faith.

The great error of the "scientific" skeptic, one that has all too frequently been made by Christian believers as well, is to think of science and Christianity as rivals, as if they were giving competing answers to the same questions. Christianity and science actually offer complementary answers to different questions.

Science tells us *what* happens in nature, and *why* it happens in the sense of *how* it happens. Christianity holds that in the Bible God reveals *who* is responsible for the natural world and *why* it exists in the sense of the ultimate *purpose* of creation.

It is simply not true that science answers all our questions about nature. For one thing, science does not tell us why the natural world exists in the first place or why it continues to exist. Scientists may trace the universe back to the original "big bang" that began the whole business, but it does not and cannot say why the big bang itself occurred. Science can explain certain events as a result of the orderly laws of nature it discovers, but it does not and cannot answer the question as to why there are orderly laws in the first place. Furthermore, science cannot answer the question as to why I as an individual exist: what is the ultimate meaning and purpose of my life?

None of these omissions represents a flaw in science. They are all questions that science must not ask, precisely to remain science and not religion.

We do not have to choose between science and Christian faith. In fact, many of the greatest scientists have been Christians, and some historians argue that it was the Christian view of the orderliness and value of nature as God's creation that made science possible in the first place.

Of course there have been and continue to be problems in reconciling particular scientific theories with the convictions of particular Christians.[1] But tensions of this sort are not necessarily unresolvable. Sometimes the tensions are due to Christians misunderstanding their faith, as was surely the case when the church condemned the theories of Galileo on the grounds that the Bible

1. An excellent book on the kinds of difficulties that have emerged historically and that still face thoughtful Christians is *The Galileo Connection: Resolving Conflicts between Science and the Bible*, by Charles Hummel (Downers Grove, IL: InterVarsity Press, 1986).

taught that the earth is the center of the universe. At other times the tension may be due to an erroneous scientific theory or, as is more common, a misinterpretation of the scope and meaning of a scientific theory. The reductionistic view of human beings as nothing but "complicated rats" that some radical behaviorists in psychology adopted for a time would be a good example of this. Honest Christians are willing to struggle with such problems, without fudging the data, because they are confident that God is the source of all truth and that the truth does not ultimately contradict itself.

A good number of present difficulties seem to revolve around the Christian doctrine of creation and the scientific theory of evolution. Many people believe that Christians must choose between believing the creation account in Genesis and accepting a scientific account of how the world and the living things in it came to be. I am not a scientist, and it is not my purpose here to evaluate the scientific theory of evolution. It should be remembered that all scientific theories are open to modification and refutation, and it is quite possible that evolutionary theory will one day be abandoned or radically modified.

Fortunately, however, Christians do not have to stake their faith on this possibility. Many Christians are convinced that evolution is simply a process God has used to create living creatures. The Genesis account is not to be taken as a detailed scientific theory; it is an account of *who* and *why,* not *how.*

This is not simply a desperate fall-back maneuver on the part of Christians. Even in the early centuries of Christianity it was recognized that the main purpose of the Genesis account is to teach us that God is responsible for the whole of nature. St. Augustine recognized, for example, that the seven "days" of creation were not literal twenty-four-hour days, but might be symbols for large periods of time. (This is especially obvious since the sun — the basis of our twenty-four-hour day — was not created until the fourth day.) Most Christians do not believe, therefore, that the universe is only a few thousand years old, nor do they think that the Bible teaches that.

But what about Adam and Eve? Doesn't the Bible teach that they were the first parents of the entire human race? Some Christians are inclined to think that Adam and Eve are not so much historical individuals but the prototypical man and woman. The story is about *us*.

But a good case can be made that Adam and Eve are intended as historical figures. Belief in a historical Adam and Eve is by no means absurd. After all, the human race clearly did have to have a *beginning*. And somewhere along the way — and why not right at the beginning? — the human race clearly began to go wrong.

It is also possible that the "dust" from which Adam and Eve were created was not literal dust, but was a symbol for evolving humanlike creatures who were finally able to be addressed by God and be held responsible. At least this is how those Christians who accept an evolutionary account of human origins view the matter. In any case there is one impressive piece of scientific evidence in favor of a common ancestry for all humans, and that is the biological unity of the entire human race. Human beings from every race and every continent share the same blood types and the same genetic structures. Recently, this evidence has gotten even stronger as scientists have studied the DNA molecules in diverse human peoples. However, even without the benefit of such scientific discoveries, it is obvious that humans can procreate together, rejoice together, and sin together.

Is God a Psychological Crutch?

A second contemporary challenge to Christian faith comes from the field of psychology. Many psychologists, Freud being the most notable, charge that religious faith is really a form of wish fulfillment. We human beings are afraid of the unfriendly powers of nature, and we are afraid of our own dark urges. To deal with these fears we postulate a "big daddy in the sky," a father who will protect us but who will also help keep us in line. Belief in God is not really rational; it's just another instance of making ourselves believe what we want to believe.

Now Freud is not completely off base here. There are genuine insights in his theory of religion, and we shall presently see how

Christians may incorporate those insights. However, the basic problem with Freud's view as a critique of Christian faith is that it commits what philosophers call the genetic fallacy, deciding the truth or falsity of a view on the basis of the origins of the view.

Take my belief that interest rates will go down soon. The "origin" of my belief may be that I need to borrow money to purchase a new car and cannot afford to pay the current high rates. This looks like — and is — a classic case of wish fulfillment. It would, however, be a fallacy for you to decide that interest rates will *not* come down simply because my reasons for believing they will are poor. Interest rates may indeed come down, and my neighbor Sam, who is an economist, may have excellent reasons for believing they will.

In a similar way many Christians may believe in God on the basis of their psychological needs. This, however, by no means implies that Christianity is false. Christianity may be true, and there may be excellent reasons for believing it is true, reasons of the sort we have tried to outline in Chapters Three through Eight. To show that Christianity is false, critics must do far more than impugn the motives of some Christians.

Actually the "psychological motive" argument cuts both ways here. We may have reasons to wish that God is real, but we also have reasons to fear that God is real and wish that he were a fantasy or projection. For if God is real, then I am ultimately accountable to him; I am not lord of my own destiny. There are many people who simply cannot bear the thought that this might be so. They say with Nietzsche (at least unconsciously), "If there were gods, how could I bear not to be a god. *Hence* there are no gods."[2] So if belief can be seen as a result of such psychological mechanisms, so can religious unbelief. Even Freud's own theory implies this, since Freud teaches that God is a "father image" and that people have a deep ambivalence toward their fathers. I know from personal experience that people who have had abusive human fathers often have difficulty relating to God as "father." If Freud's psychology is right, then many of us harbor unconscious anger at

2. Friedrich Nietzsche, *Thus Spoke Zarathustra,* second part, ed. and trans. Walter Kaufmann, in *The Portable Nietzsche* (New York: Viking, 1968), 198.

our fathers, and it is logical that some of this resentment would transfer to God.

Actually it is not always unreasonable to allow beliefs to be affected by our needs and wishes. All of us have a fundamental need to believe that our experience is reliable; ought we to distrust the belief on those grounds? It is not obvious that *all* beliefs can or should be formed in a strictly logical manner, simply by evaluating evidence.

As I noted in Chapter Six, many Christians are inclined to think that Freud is right in saying that humans have a fundamental need to believe in God. What Freud failed to see is that the reason this may be true is that God has created us to enjoy communion with himself. God is our ultimate, deepest need. We need to believe in him because we need *him,* and God created us this way. And, again as argued in Chapter Six, this kind of need may itself be powerful evidence for God's reality. Even the Freudian point that our ideas of God are formed from our fathers is not really hostile to Christianity. For Christians believe that God created families — fathers and mothers — and one of his reasons for doing so may well have been to help us gain a better understanding of himself and our relation to him.

Is Christianity Sexist?

The Freudian charge that belief in God is linked to the need for a father brings to mind another accusation commonly heard on university campuses and among intellectuals generally today: that Christianity is sexist. There is no question that the dominant traditional images of God in Christianity have been masculine: God is often referred to as king and lord, as well as father. Many feminists argue that religion in general and Christianity in particular are inextricably tied to the oppression of women. They argue that when "God is male, then the male is God" and see a link between what they call "patriarchal" religious beliefs and hierarchical, patriarchal societies.

I think most fair-minded people would recognize that most

human societies have been sexist, and that sexism remains a serious problem today. Over the centuries women have been regarded as male property and denied equal legal protection. They have often been forced to do a disproportionate share of the burdensome work of society, and their contributions have been under-recognized and under-rewarded. Though some legal progress has been made in most Western societies, women still suffer enormously from economic discrimination, rape, and abuse in families, which is most often directed by males against females. In many families women still do a disproportionate share of the work in cleaning, cooking, and child rearing, even when, as is now usually the case, women work outside the home. All of these problems in turn reflect deeply ingrained attitudes that many men harbor towards women, consciously or unconsciously.

Honesty compels Christians to admit that such sexism has been prevalent among Christians in the church, just as in society generally. Christian churches have usually reflected and often even encouraged the sexism of their culture, just as they have often reflected and sometimes encouraged such cultural evils as nationalism and racism.

Despite these melancholy truths, which must be clearly faced, I wish to claim that Christianity is not inherently sexist. Rather, it is Christian insights that have made possible the recognition that sexism is a great evil. The message of Christianity is essentially one of liberation for women.

How is it possible to make such a claim while admitting that Christians have struggled greatly in this area and often failed? The answer to this question lies in the Christian doctrine of sin. The Bible is a most realistic book, and its picture of human life is one that is unfortunately all too commonly verified by the continued cruelty of humans to each other. The picture is one of a fallen race. On the Christian view, the human rebellion against God is a rebellion that has spoiled and distorted every aspect of human life. Sin pervades both individual human hearts and the social institutions constructed by humans.

This biblical picture of sin is not the usual Hollywood theme of "good guys versus the bad guys," or "us against them." That is, it would be a radical mistake for Christians to think of themselves as essentially good and other people as "sinners." Rather, the Christian view is that "all have sinned." Christians are not Christians by virtue of being especially good; they are forgiven sinners. And though God's forgiveness certainly should make a difference in the way Christians live, there is no reason to think that the changes will be complete or instantaneous. The church is composed of sinners, and must always be aware of the possibility and even the reality of sin within the ranks. That is why most churches embody ongoing confession of sin as part of their worship services.

When one considers the near-universal and often unnoticed character of sexism, it is hardly surprising that a church of redeemed sinners would struggle with this issue. The example of slavery is very instructive here. The Bible does not clearly call for the abolition of slavery as an institution, and in societies such as the pre–Civil War American South, where slavery was a central economic institution, most churches defended the institution as right. The churches reflected and often tried to justify an institution that most people today would recognize as evil.

Nevertheless, it is no accident that the leaders of the anti-slavery movement were largely inspired by Christian faith, because there is at the heart of Christian faith a conviction that is incompatible with human slavery: the conviction that all human beings are created by God and gain their ultimate worth and value from their status as creatures made in God's image. In the time of the New Testament, slavery was an entrenched social institution and there was no realistic hope for its overthrow. The writers of the New Testament did not endorse utopian, unrealistic schemes for social and political change. They did, however, clearly proclaim a message that ultimately was to lead to the abolition of slavery. This is the message that God created all human beings in his image and that Jesus of Nazareth as the Son of God died for all those human beings: male and female, slave and free, Jew and Greek.

The seeds of the destruction of slavery can be clearly seen in Paul's letter in the New Testament to a slaveholder named Philemon, urging Philemon to welcome back an escaped slave. Though Paul does not attack the institution of slavery politically, he says clearly that the slaveholder must receive his former slave as a brother in Christ, and such an attitude seems incompatible with regarding a human being simply as property to be bought and sold.

The issue of slavery is more than an illustration of how a social evil can be incompatible with Christian faith though tolerated and even endorsed by Christians for a long time. For the central Christian message that led to the abolition of slavery is the very message that ultimately stands at the bottom of the condemnation of sexism.

It is worth asking how we know that sexism is wrong. It is certainly not obvious that one would come to recognize the evil of sexism simply by looking at the inherited moral traditions of various cultures, for most of these traditions seem to endorse the idea of male superiority. Even so humane and astute a philosopher as Aristotle found the superiority of men to women to be entirely natural. If we ask how and why the equality of women and men has come to be widely recognized, I believe the answer lies squarely in the biblical conviction that men and women are created in God's image. As was the case with slavery, the implications of this idea have been very slow to be recognized and even slower to be implemented, but nonetheless the idea is already present in the Genesis account of creation, which, after affirming that God created human beings in his image, spells out and reinforces the meaning of this by affirming that human beings were created "male and female."[3]

The origins of the idea that women and men are equally and fully human do not lie solely in the doctrine of creation in the image of God. The attitude and practice of Jesus towards women has also been of decisive importance. It is important to realize that women were definitely second-class members of society in first-century Palestine. A woman was legally a minor and could only be divorced at her husband's request. Women could not enter into

3. See Genesis 1:27. The structure of this verse, which employs Hebrew parallelism, in which a second clause repeats in a somewhat different manner the meaning of a first clause, implies that the image of God actually consists in or is at least closely tied to the fact that God created human beings as male and female.

the more central parts of the temple. They were not taught the Torah as men were. In light of this, Jesus' behavior towards women can only be viewed as remarkable.[4]

Jesus shocked even his own disciples by being alone with a Samaritan woman of dubious moral reputation, and asking of her a drink, which would make him ritually unclean; he revealed himself to this woman as the Messiah (John 4:7-42). Jesus did not condemn a woman caught in adultery, but saved her life, asking her only to sin no more (John 8:3-11). When Jesus was "defiled" by being touched with a woman with a hemorrhage, he commended the faith of the woman and healed her (Matt. 9:20-22). Jesus accepted the love and kisses of a woman who was a "sinner" and who shamed herself by letting down her hair to wipe his feet, and told the woman that her sins were forgiven because she had "loved much" (Luke 7:36-50). It is clear that many of his closest followers were women and that they provided not only encouragement but financial support for his ministry. It is noteworthy that women were the first witnesses to the resurrection.

It is not surprising then that this revolutionary attitude towards women continued to be reflected in the early church. Women were accepted as prophets and teachers, and many of the Apostle Paul's close coworkers were women. It is true that Paul sometimes stressed the need for recognizing traditional roles. Society cannot be totally transformed overnight, and Paul no more called for the abolition of all traditional sexual roles than he called for the abolition of slavery. Nevertheless, the overall thrust of Paul's teaching is clearly that men and women are equally children of God in Christ: "So there is no difference between Jews and Gentiles, between slaves and free men, between men and women; you are all one in union with Christ Jesus" (Gal. 3:28).

The use of male images for God does not mean that God is literally male. Traditional Christian theology has always clearly maintained that God has no body and is neither male nor female. When Jesus calls God "Father" *(Abba)* the point is not to reinforce

---

4. The following summary of Jesus' behavior towards women draws heavily on the well-written summary of Elaine Storkey in *What's Right With Feminism* (Grand Rapids: Wm. B. Eerdmans, 1985), 156-59.

the authority of a human patriarch, but to provide a transformed understanding of God, an understanding that in turn can be the basis for a transformed understanding of what it means to be a human father. Elaine Storkey captures this insight beautifully:

> [W]e call God "Father" because Christ invited us to. And here again, Jesus is not making a point about God's "gender," . . . but is using the word to tell us about the kind of relationship we might have. We might have this intimate, gentle, caring relationship from one who loves, protects, cuddles, feeds and nourishes us. For the word "Abba" is nothing like the word used to describe a patriarch. It is simply "daddy." Jesus then is inviting us to share his daddy, to come to the relationship with someone who watches our every move, cares about our every tear, and knows exactly where it hurts. To reduce the deep intimacy of this fatherly (and motherly) relationship into fear of a male God is to distance oneself from the source of real self-knowledge and full womanly identity.[5]

There are clearly forms of radical feminism that are incompatible with historic Christian belief. Christianity cannot accept the idea, for example, of the "androgynous ideal," in which no differences between men and women are acknowledged, for Christians hold that it is no accident that God created human beings as male and female. Christianity draws a sharp line between the worship of the transcendent God, who made heaven and earth, and the neopagan worship of "the goddess" modeled on ancient fertility goddesses that some radical feminists have advocated. So although Christian faith is clearly at odds with some of the ideas advocated by such radicals, it is solidly behind the idea that men and women are equally created in God's image and the object of Christ's love. It is no accident that many of the pioneers of the feminist movement in the nineteenth century who led the fight for the right to vote and women's equality were Christian social reformers.

5. Storkey, 126.

Is God the Opiate of the People?

Another challenge to Christian faith is posed by sociologists and political theorists, particularly by Marxists and others who are committed to radical political and social changes. Political radicals often see belief in God as an impediment to social progress. They see belief in God as a way of sanctifying or "baptizing" the political and economic status quo. We may no longer believe in the "divine right of kings," but we all too often see the current establishment as God's will. Those who suffer and are oppressed shouldn't resist God. In any case, they will be rewarded and compensated for their sufferings in another life: "Pie in the sky by and by."

Once more, as was the case with Freud, this type of criticism at bottom commits the genetic fallacy. If God is real, he is real, even if some people believe in him (or get others to believe in him) for lousy political reasons. If God exists, then people should believe the truth, whether the truth has social and political consequences that are favorable or unfavorable.

However, we must not dismiss this kind of critique too quickly. As was also the case with Freud, there are genuine insights here that could and should be accepted by Christians. The idea that religious faith can be misused for social, political, and economic oppression is by no means news to the Christian, and of course we have already encountered this sad truth in our look at the question of whether Christianity is sexist. The Bible is full of accounts of religion being misused to further various political and economic agendas. It is equally full of God's denunciations of this practice.

The Old Testament prophets constantly denounce those who practice injustice and think that their religious practices will some-how excuse this or cover it over.[6] God makes it clear through his prophets that real worship cannot coexist with injustice and op-pression. God wants obedience to his commands, not merely empty ceremonies. And God is a God who cares about the poor and the oppressed, who takes the cause of the widow and the fatherless.

6. See Micah 3:5; 6:6-8; Isaiah 29:13; Ezekiel 13:10; and Jeremiah 5:31 for examples of these denunciations.

Jesus denounces the religious establishment of his day in much the same way and for much the same reasons (Mark 12:40).

Christians can agree with political radicals, then, that religion is often misused for selfish human purposes. We are only too anxious to claim that God is on our side, and not nearly anxious enough as to whether we are really on God's side. But the fact that Christianity is misused by sinful human beings is not very surprising to Christians.

The reason that it is possible for any religion to be misused in this way is that religious beliefs do have social consequences. This is important to recognize, for there is a widespread assumption that Christianity concerns only the "spiritual" realm and has nothing to do with politics and economics.

This view of Christianity is a serious distortion. The correct insight that the distortion feeds on is that Christianity does teach that the ultimate solution to human problems lies in knowing God and that this is not reducible to any social or political program. A Christian's ultimate allegiance must be to God and the principles of his kingdom: love and justice. Particular political and economic programs, whether capitalistic or socialistic, can be partially and provisionally accepted only insofar as they contribute to these kingdom goals. (Which of course is consistent with Christianity holding that some political programs are clearly superior to others.)

There is a revolutionary aspect to Christian faith; the fact that true Christians must never give their total and ultimate allegiance to any human entity means that Christians can never be counted on to be completely compliant to any human authority. It is doubtless for this reason that totalitarian regimes are usually quick to abolish freedom of religion. Nevertheless, despite the fact that Christianity cannot be identified with any particular political program, Christian faith is far from being a purely "private" affair. Christian faith should transform the whole person. It has implications for every area of life.

This can be seen from the history of the church. Christians have certainly not all been reactionaries. Many have been at the forefront of progressive social movements. The abolitionist attack on slavery was largely led by Christians and was inspired by Christian ideals from start to finish. We have already noted that many of the pioneers of the nineteenth-century movement for women's suffrage and equality were Christians. The civil rights movement in this century was launched from the pulpits of black Christian ministers. Christians in Latin America today are struggling to apply their faith in situations characterized by vast extremes of wealth and poverty and tremendous human suffering. Even Marxists in Latin America have been forced to recognize that Christian faith can be a force for justice.

There are also many tragic cases of failure, where Christian ideals have been only selectively applied or have been hypocritically accepted in a purely verbal way. One example that is somewhat less sordid, perhaps, than others, but even more damaging to the faith of many, is the effect of much so-called religious television. As Hank Williams, Jr., sings, "Some preachers on TV . . . tell you to send your money to the Lord, but they give you their address." But Christians do not claim to be perfect. They are finite, sinful human beings, redeemed by Christ and not by their own good works. The example of a Mother Teresa may be a powerful aid to faith, but Christian faith is faith in Christ, not in Christians.

Christianity, "Religion," and the Church

There is no question that a lot of horrible things are done in the name of "religion." In Northern Ireland and in the Middle East, religion has become an excuse to hate and to kill. In the name of "religion" huckstering con artists get sincere older people to give away their life savings. People use religion to justify bigotry and racism. A look back into history reveals that almost every imaginable crime has been justified by religion.

But is Christianity a religion in this sense? It depends on how the term is defined. In one sense of the word Christianity is undeniably a religion. Like other religions, it has millions of adherents, and many organizations and institutions. It resembles other religions in many interesting respects (including being used to justify one's own favorite causes, whether they be worthy or unworthy), and is different from the others in many interesting ways as well.

One definition of a religion is that it is a "human attempt to relate to God." Using this definition, Christianity is undoubtedly a religion. Christians are human, and they do try to relate to God. However, if Christianity is true, it is not *merely* a religion in this sense. Christianity claims that it is not up to us to get to know God and relate to him. God has taken the initiative. In Christ he has made it possible for us to get to know him. The Bible is not so much a record of our attempts to get to know God, but of God's prolonged courtship of us.

Christians believe that God's action in Christ is not merely "religion." It is God's work, and that work is still going on through Christ's "body," the church. It's true that a lot of what the church does, including perhaps some of the things that get the most publicity, is merely "religion." However, here and there, wherever Christians are faithful to their Lord and led by the spirit of Christ, the work of God is being done.

The implications of this are simple. Christians do not have to defend everything that is done in the name of religion, even what is done in the name of the Christian religion. Many people have obstructed and opposed genuine science in the name of religion. Many people have used religion to justify or sanctify unjust or corrupt institutions and actions. Rather than defend these things, Christians should be the first to oppose them. What they must not do is to allow any of this to be equated with God's work in the world.

The Christian's calling is not to advance the cause of religion. It is to advance the kingdom of God. The people who have been called by God in Jesus Christ to do this work are called the church. The church is a vital part of the Christian message, because the call of Christ is not a call to individualism, but a call to togetherness. No one can be a Christian in isolation.

To be a part of the church certainly means that Christians will identify with particular, concrete groups. They will build buildings, plan programs, and promote denominations and organizations. However, none of these things *is* the church, and it is sometimes perilously easy to confuse the means with the end. What must be remembered is simply this: the church is the people of God; its mission is to obediently serve its Lord and work for his kingdom.

CHAPTER TWELVE

Good News and Bad News

Lies and romances must be probable . . . , but not the truth and fundamental doctrine of our Faith.

Johann Georg Hamann, Letter to his brother

God does not die on the day we cease to believe in a personal deity, but we die on the day when our lives cease to be illumined by the steady radiance, renewed daily, of a wonder, the source of which is beyond all reason.

Dag Hammarskjöld, *Markings*

MANY PEOPLE THINK that being a Christian is very difficult. Others think that it is extremely easy. Both groups are right, but very often they are wrong about the real reasons for the difficulty and for the ease. The good news is that what seems hard is easy. The bad news is that what seems easy is terribly difficult.

Many people believe Christianity is difficult because it is a religion with impossibly high moral and ethical standards. It is true that Christians are asked to do many things that go against what seems natural to us in our present state of rebellion against God. We are asked to love our neighbors as ourselves and told

121

that even our enemy is our neighbor. (Of course this love is not a mushy immediate feeling — such feelings cannot be commanded — but a determination to *act* for the good of our neighbor and to work at developing appropriate emotional attitudes.) We are asked to place God and his kingdom — his values — higher in our affections than any earthly good — money, power, prestige, security, or even the joys of family life. We are told that we must be willing to suffer for the sake of righteousness.

It is quite true that these things are not easy. In fact there is a sense in which they are impossible. They are impossible so long as we try to live our lives independently of God. The virtues that God demands cannot be achieved apart from his help.

This is why it is crucial to see that Christianity is not simply a moral or ethical code. A person does not become a Christian by deciding to live in accordance with Christian morality. Rather, becoming a Christian is a matter of coming to know God and share in his life. This is what is offered us in Christ: *new life*. This is why from the beginning Christianity has insisted that to become a follower of Christ is to be "born again."

The new life in Christ is not something that must be earned or willed; it is a *gift*. Growth in the Christian life is a matter of realizing this more and more profoundly. This is why humility and gratitude are so fundamental. Even if a Christian is leading an exceptionally moral life, she is going in the wrong direction if she does not understand herself to be continuously dependent on God.

Fundamentally, what God asks from us is simple: he wants us to turn from our selfishness, self-centeredness, and self-assurance, and center our selves in him. In return he offers us a new self and new life. It is true that he intends to change us radically, to make us the sort of people who are willing to love our enemies and share our worldly goods with the poor. But it's not as if we must first live up to his standards and then become his children. All he asks from us is that we be willing to become his children. The changes he wants to make in us will come eventually from the new life he will put in us. The process may take a long time, but God seems to have a great deal of patience.

Put that way, it sounds easy, not hard at all. Yet in a way this simple act of learning to trust God, to depend on him and build our lives around him (which is what Christians call faith), is what is really difficult. We would prefer to retain our independence. Some people declare their independence by rebelling against God. Others are willing to try to please him, but they also do this in a way that maintains their independence. They may work desperately hard at this, but they fail to see that God's fundamental desire for his children is that they recognize that they are his children and accept his fatherly (and motherly) love. He is a parent whom we please not by showing our ability to brilliantly live up to difficult rules, but by returning to him in childlike faith.

This paradoxical blend of difficulty and ease pervades all of the Christian life. It is present not only in the practical day-to-day struggles, but in the most fundamental Christian beliefs about God.

It is a notorious fact that some of the most basic Christian beliefs — those convictions the church calls doctrines — are complicated, hard to understand, and difficult to believe. Christians believe in one God, as do Jews and Muslims, but they believe that this one God exists in three persons. Christians believe that the man Jesus, who was born of a simple maiden from Galilee, was the God who had made the world and purposed from all eternity to redeem his fallen race. Christians believe that this same Jesus will someday return to this earth to establish a glorious kingdom and that all those who love him will be bodily raised from the dead to enjoy everlasting life. Certainly these things (and others) *are* mysterious. But should they be a barrier to becoming a Christian?

True Stories and Cunning Fables

Suppose you wanted to invent a religion. Several motives for such a thing can be imagined. You might sincerely think that people could be improved. Or maybe you just want to be high priest or pope or general secretary.

In any case, how would you do it? Most likely you would formulate very appealing doctrines, ideas that would strike most people as reasonable, even obviously true. In this way your own credibility as a prophet of sorts would be boosted.

One thing is certain. This is *not* what the earliest Christians did. If Peter and John and Paul and the other apostles wanted to invent a new religion, they could hardly have hit on doctrines less plausible to their hearers. To the strictly monotheistic Jews they proclaimed that Jesus was the Son of God and that Jesus and his father were both God. To the rationalistic Greeks they proclaimed that Jesus, lock, stock, and body, had risen from the dead and that his followers would someday experience this same resurrection.

It is obvious that the apostles were not devising cunning fables. The very preposterousness of their teachings is a sign that they were proclaiming what they had experienced as true and were convinced was true. Only hard reality could have brought them to make the claims they did.

The church is still very much in the position of the early apostles. Although there are always "modern thinkers" who would like to reshape the message a little to make it more palatable, genuine Christians have always recognized that the message such people proclaim is ultimately not the Christian message. Christians are not at liberty to develop a "new, improved version" because the gospel is not a story of their own making. Truth is sometimes complicated. Truth *is* often stranger than fiction, and the reason for this is simple. Good fiction must be plausible; it must meet our expectations as to how things are. Reality, however, is not under the same obligation. It can and does surprise us.

A first and fundamental point, then, is simply this: the fact that basic Christian doctrines are complicated, hard to understand, and even hard to believe does not prove them false. It rather is a sign that these teachings stemmed from people who were not inventing cunning fables, but trying to describe the truth as they had experienced it.

The second, equally fundamental point about the basic Christian doctrines is this: they are not simply doctrines, they are mysteries. It is not the critics of Christianity who discovered that these basic Christian teachings were difficult to understand and hard to believe. The church itself has always taught, and even insisted on, this. From the perspective of human reason, the teachings always have been and continue to be mysteries.

In calling these basic doctrines mysteries, Christianity means several things. Among the most important of these is that these teachings are only known to be true through a special, divine revelation. They are not something which human reason could ever have discovered, and even when they have been revealed, they are not something reason can simply appropriate for its own.

Now it is true that reason very often tries to use this fact as an objection against Christian faith. "I can't make any sense of these things," says Reason. "They're just absurd." To which Faith replies, "Of course they look absurd to you if you try to understand them relying purely on your own efforts. These are God's mysteries, which he has graciously made known to us."

To see the strength of Faith's reply, suppose that God has given a special revelation to us. What would we expect such a revelation to contain? Commonsense advice such as "Dress warmly in cold weather"? We would hardly need a special revelation from God to know that. Fundamental truths of mathematics and science? Perhaps God could make our lives easier by revealing such things, but then he would be denying us the opportunity to develop our minds by making such discoveries ourselves.

Perhaps we might expect a true special revelation from God to contain wise, moral teachings. This is more plausible, and indeed, the Bible arguably contains the deepest ethical teachings to be found in all human history. Nevertheless, a great deal of that teaching is paralleled in the teachings of the sages of other religions and cultures. In any case, once biblical ethics is known, a good deal of it can be philosophically defended as reasonable. Thus it looks as if wise, moral teachings, while perhaps one of the things we would expect to find in a special revelation from God, are the sort of thing that could be found in a merely human work. They are not a sure sign of divine authority.

If God were going to give humans a special revelation, it should contain some truth that humans would be unable to discover on their own. Otherwise, why would he bother? In other words, we would expect a *genuine* revelation from God to contain mysteries. It would be surprising indeed if a true revelation from God contained nothing that was mysterious to finite, sinful human beings. The fact that Christianity contains doctrines that are mysteries is therefore precisely what we would expect if Christianity is, as it claims to be, rooted in a special revelation from God.

Of course if we crave autonomy, the fact that Christianity presents mysteries that are rooted in a special revelation from God is indeed a barrier to our faith. It is a great blow against our self-sufficiency, a shock to our claims of independence. It is one way God forcibly reminds us that we need him and that we can return to him only by acknowledging that he is God and we are not. Accepting a mystery on the basis of authority is hard.

But the difficulty is the same basic difficulty that is always present in the life of faith. It is hard to surrender, even to a loving father. Yet it is easy, too, for those who are humble and honest enough to recognize their need for God. To those who have come home, these mysteries are the delightful and intriguing hints God has disclosed about himself and the new life he offers to his children. Of course they are the sort of thing I could never have thought of on my own! Of course they are the sort of thing I cannot even now fully understand! They are mysteries that God has revealed.

A wise Christian should therefore never try to defend the faith by making God's mysteries into plausible human inventions. Christian doctrines are not philosophical theories to be logically proven. Nevertheless, a valid role for human thought remains if it is willing to entertain the need for a revelation and the possibility that God might provide one.

Christians have usually insisted that the basic mysteries of the faith are *above* reason, but not *against* reason. That is, although we cannot fully understand them or prove their truth, they do not contradict what *is* known to be truth. (Though they may contradict what seems true, especially to people who insist that their own reason is essentially infallible, or an all-sufficient source of truth.)

Thus reason can be helpful in showing that these mysteries do not contradict what is known to be true. In doing so, reason can often help us gain a clearer perspective on what we believe. Our understanding may never in this life be perfectly clear, since we always "see through a glass darkly." But it is often helpful to employ our imaginations to gain a clearer, if still less than complete, sense of what God wants to teach us.

Three Persons in One

Why should God want to reveal mysteries to us? Surely not to excite our curiosity or stimulate us to develop new research programs in theology. The mysteries God reveals would be things that are vital for us to know. The knowledge would be practical. God wishes us to know things about himself and his plans for us so that we may properly relate to him.

This is precisely the case with the basic Christian doctrine of the Trinity. God is one God, yet he exists as Father, Son, and Holy Spirit. Clearly this is a mystery. We cannot fathom such a being. Perhaps with the help of various analogies we can get a vague sense of what such a being must be like and why we cannot fully understand it. (Could a two-dimensional being fully understand what a three-dimensional being would be like?)

Why then do Christians believe that the one God is Father, Son, and Holy Spirit? The reason is that this is how the earliest Christians experienced God. God had already revealed himself as Creator, the almighty, holy Being who called humans back to himself. Then a man named Jesus appeared, a sane man who made convincing claims to be God, yet who as a human clearly prayed to God as father. After Jesus left the earth, these same Christians experienced God within them. God was beyond them, had been beside them, and now was within them. The early Christians found that in all these situations they were experiencing the same God, and yet the distinctions between God as Father, Son, and Spirit were nonetheless real. These were the hard experiences that gave rise to the doctrine of the Trinity.

These are the same experiences that are offered to us today. We have a more or less clear idea of God, the almighty Creator. Most people believe in him, though a few do not, and virtually everyone understands the idea. As we have seen in Chapters Two through Four, we can become aware of God's reality through the calling cards he has left in the physical universe and human nature.

This God is a God who is fully revealed in Jesus, a Jesus who is more than a prophet, but in some way is himself identical with the Father. Jesus is God "focused" in human form, a God whom we can clearly know and follow. Jesus points us to God the Father, but at the same time we come to know the Father by knowing the Son.

Finally, as we turn to God in Jesus we discover God within us. The Spirit of the Father and Son is present, giving us new interests and affections, changing our whole view of life and ourselves. The Trinity is not a speculative theory, but an invitation to participate in the life of God in a way we would never have imagined.

Though the Trinity is not a speculative theory, and though it admittedly exceeds our intellectual comprehension, there is nonetheless something fitting about the whole notion. One way of putting this is to say that the Trinity implies that God is more than personal. There are many people who are critical of the idea of a personal God. The idea of personality is too limiting to attribute to God, they say.

Unfortunately, these critics of the idea of a personal God, which is so basic to Christianity, Judaism, and Islam, invariably wind up substituting an idea of something that is less than personal for the idea of God as personal. God is seen as a cosmic force, or the ground of being, or as natural law. Only Christianity proposes that God is somehow more than personal, that he is three while yet remaining essentially one.

In saying that God is more personal, I am not saying that he is impersonal. God transcends personhood as *we* experience it. But the truth is probably that God is personal in a truer and deeper way than we can understand. Part of what this means, I think, is that God is fundamentally *social*. If there is one thing about us that seems sure, it is that we are not islands or isolated atoms. We are what we are and become what we become because of our relations to other persons. Just try to imagine yourself independently of your parents and friends. Whether you have imitated them or rebelled against them, you have become what you have become through your relations with them.

The doctrine of the Trinity implies that God is social in his very being. Even apart from his creation, God is and always was a community, a community characterized by perfect love and unity yet utter respect for distinctions. God perfectly embodies that diversity-in-unity that human communities at their best strive to attain. Almost everyone knows that Christianity teaches that God is love. Yet it is only the doctrine of the Trinity that allows for love to be the most fundamental fact about the inner life of God.

Incarnation

We have already laid out the case (in Chapters Seven and Eight) for the fundamental claim that Jesus was the unique son of God. This claim is certainly hard to understand and difficult to believe. That is partly why it *is* believable. If a person claims to be God, then if the claim isn't true, the person must be either a lunatic or an unscrupulous charlatan. Jesus, however, seems perfectly sane, and not even his bitterest enemies have ever accused him of being a moral monster. Only one option remains: Jesus really is divine, just as he claimed to be.

How can an individual human being be God? I do not pretend to know. We must remember that we are dealing here with mysteries that by definition surpass the powers of human reason. The claim is not, however, impossible to believe.

One point in favor of the possibility of an incarnation of God is the fact that we resemble God. The Bible teaches that God made us in his own image. Though God differs vastly from us in the scope of his knowledge and power, nevertheless both God and we are personal. As persons, we are self-conscious, capable of acting and knowing. The notion that God became flesh (became human) may be staggering, but it is not absurd in the way it would be to claim that God had become a rock or an oak tree.

Any attempts to help us understand how an incarnation might be possible will, I think, make heavy use of the simple word *as*. All of us do things at one time that we cannot do at others. I can discipline my child *as* a parent, write a check *as* an account-holder at my bank, hire an employee *as* a supervisor. These analogies cannot be pushed since they are vastly different than the Incarnation. Nevertheless, we can, I think, attach some sense to the notion that Jesus is God *as* a human. Jesus is *as* God the Creator of all things other than himself, the all-mighty, all-knowing One. Jesus

is *as* a human a particular person, who experienced human finitude. He knew what it was like to be cold, hungry, and tired.

One way of thinking about this that I have found helpful is
to recognize that *God* is not merely a name for a class or type
of being, but the name of an individual. The biblical God is a
particular person who called Abram out of Ur and gave the Ten
Commandments to Moses. Now a particular individual can assume a new role and function, take on new characteristics, and
(perhaps temporarily) choose to relinquish or not to exercise
certain characteristics without ceasing to be the particular individual he or she is. The New Testament suggests that something
like this happened in the case of Jesus. Though he was God from
all eternity, he "emptied himself," choosing to leave aside some
of the characteristics he possessed *as* God, but without ceasing
to *be* God, the particular individual he was.[1] Of course all of this
must be taken in conjunction with the doctrine of the Trinity,
since if there is no "plurality" in God then the Incarnation seems
truly impossible.

Atonement and Redemption

Sometimes Christians and would-be Christians are bothered not
by the doctrine of the Incarnation itself, but by the doctrines of
atonement and redemption. Christians believe that Jesus, in his
death and resurrection, atoned, or made amends, for the sins of
human beings. He paid the price of sin for us and then triumphed
over sin and death, which is the outcome of sin.

This is often explained in terms of a theory of "substitutionary
atonement." Jesus was an innocent victim, who took the punishment we deserved and thereby satisfied God's demand for a just
penalty.

The first thing that must be said about this is that it is the
fact of atonement that Christians are asked to believe, not any
particular *theory* as to how this is achieved by Christ's death and

1. See Philippians 2:7.

resurrection. Indeed, Christians have over the centuries held a variety of theories about how this occurred. The substitutionary theory was not clearly formulated until Anselm did so in the eleventh century A.D. So if you do not find a theory of how God accomplished your redemption in Christ helpful, do not let that be a barrier to believing that he has done so.

Nevertheless, the substitutionary theory has and has had wide support in the church. The image of "substitution" is often used in Scripture, along with others, of course. The problem with this theory is, I think, that it often is presented in an overly legalistic manner. God the Father is the stern lawgiver who imposes a punishment on Jesus, the innocent victim, so that he will not have to pour out his wrath on the rest of us. The whole business sounds like a cold, legal transaction.

What is forgotten in this picture is that Christians are monotheists as well as Trinitarians. God the Father and God the Son are one. When Jesus gives his life for us, it is not God punishing an innocent victim, but God giving himself for us. In the death and resurrection of Jesus, God shows us how complete his love for us is. He fully assumes our guilt — even experiencing death — and through his sacrifice overcomes guilt and death. The real mystery here is not "How did God atone for sin?" It is the mystery of the unfathomable divine love that shows itself in his atoning actions.

The following story, adapted from philosopher Eleonore Stump, may help to illumine the idea of atonement. Imagine that a mother has a beautiful garden that she dearly loves. Her son has been warned not to play soccer around the garden, but he disregards her instructions and tears the garden to shreds. Of course the really difficult thing for the mother is not the disturbed garden, but the lack of love on the part of her son. The son's actions have created a breach in their relation.

How can the breach be overcome and the relationship restored? If the son was sorry for his action, perhaps the mother could forgive him. Of course the son, if he was truly sorry, might want to make amends by restoring the garden. If he was too small and unskilled to do this, we can easily imagine the mother helping him, perhaps restoring a key section herself. Such costly love on

her part would undoubtedly increase the son's love and apprecia-
tion for the mother.

Of course if the son wasn't even sorry for his deed, then the
mother's task would be even more difficult. Should she simply
forgive him by ignoring the action and pretending it did not happen? Such "forgiveness" would not really reestablish the relationship, because it would mean that the mother did not really take
the son's actions seriously. Perhaps the best solution would again
be for the mother to offer the son forgiveness by repairing the
damage herself. Perhaps when the son saw the mother on her hands
and knees, suffering the consequences that by right he should be
suffering, he would be moved to love her and to join in her work.
By suffering on his behalf the mother would graciously tell him
that all will be well — he is forgiven and she is herself making
amends for his misdeed.

Of course the story does not work if understood in strictly
legal terms. How can the mother make amends for her son to
herself? But families don't operate on a strictly legal basis. The
mother is willing to forgive, and to forgive in a costly way that
shows she takes the son's wrong actions seriously.

Christians believe that is what God is like. He takes us seriously and cannot simply ignore our destructive actions, our lack
of love for himself and each other. He is willing to forgive and
renew those who truly are sorry for the misguided paths they are
traveling and want to change directions. But part of the problem
is that we aren't really sorry; we don't want to change directions.
Here God reaches out to us by "atoning," making amends for us.
He takes on human form and suffers the consequences of sin,
expressing both the seriousness with which he views our sin and
the exuberant love with which he is willing to forgive our sins. He
undoes the damage and conquers sin by suffering the death that
is the consequence of sin.

The problem of guilt remains a major problem for contemporary people. Though we try to reduce the problem to one of
guilt-*feelings* (and there are people who feel guilty when they are
not), the best human beings are precisely those who refuse the
smug sense of moral superiority or the easy justification of oneself
as being "as good as the next person." Morally sensitive people

struggle with whether they are doing all they should in the face of the sufferings of others. The Christian doctrine of atonement is far from being an outdated moral concept. It provides a way of dealing with guilt that takes the moral demand seriously without the need for self-deception about our own lives. Atonement implies that we can be fully honest with ourselves because we can be fully honest with God. It does not mean never having to say you are sorry, but being able to say you are sorry. God accepts us and forgives us as we are, without trivializing our moral debts or our broken relationships.

If you cannot fully understand why God could do this or how he could do this, take comfort. The critical question is not whether you fully understand God's action in suffering on your behalf. It is whether you are moved by his suffering to "turn around," to repent. Then the power of God that conquered death in Jesus will be at work in your life as well.

The Resurrection of the Body and the Life Everlasting

But has Jesus really conquered death? Is the notion of life after death believable today?

Of course if human beings are purely physical creatures, fully understandable as matter in motion, the idea of life after death is absurd. A person would cease to be when the body ceased to be.

We are not, however, purely physical creatures. We know that in our hearts, even when we deny it. Our sense that we are more than bodies expresses itself even in our language. We say of a person who has just died that he has gone; he is no longer there. We sense that in burying a corpse we are not burying the person we knew and loved; she is no longer here.

The identity of a human being is not found merely by looking at the body as a physical object. I am who I am because of my thoughts, feelings, actions, memories, and other rich elements of consciousness, which form my personal history. Even in this life I am not simply a physical object; the atoms that compose my body are constantly changing, yet my "person" remains. Christians have traditionally affirmed this truth that we are more than physical objects by speaking of people as *souls* and *spirits* as well as *bodies*.

These notions of soul and spirit have acquired confusing and misleading meanings that make it difficult for us today to accept them. Too many people think of the soul as a ghost that resides somewhere *in* the body. As scientists repeatedly find no ghosts in our bodies, it becomes harder to believe in souls.

However, to speak of soul and spirit is not to speak of a ghost residing in a person. It is to speak of the person himself (or herself) — that essential core that makes us persons. Christians are very clear that we are meant to be embodied. In this life and in our ultimate intended state after death, personhood is expressed in bodily form; it is incarnated. But our personhood can survive the death of our present bodies. The power of God, which gives us life now, can continue our conscious, personal history in a new body. It seems odd that people who watch *Star Trek* and are familiar with "teletransporters" that dematerialize a person in one place and then rematerialize that person as a bodily being in a remote place would claim to find this idea of God recreating us as bodily beings unintelligible.

Life after death is not as strange in an age of computers as many think. Some materialistic philosophers like to think of human beings as computers of a particular type, using synapses in the brain instead of silicon circuits. Some of them seriously think that someday we will have computers who are real "persons." I personally doubt this is so, and I think it is a mistake to regard persons as a kind of computer, or any future computers as persons. However, though computers are not persons, if we wished to think of persons by using computer metaphors, we would be better off thinking of persons as "software with a history" than simply as hardware. We are more like "running programs" (though unique, individual programs) than machines. It is a commonplace that a computer program (with suitable modifications at times) can be run on very different machines. In the same way God can surely continue our personal histories in new bodies. Thus even the machine analogies that the materialist would like to use to deny life after death end up supporting the possibility.

Doctrines and Authority

This book is not a textbook in Christian doctrine or systematic theology. Thus I have made no attempt comprehensively to survey the whole of Christian doctrine or deal with all the problems suggested by particular Christian themes. Rather, I have merely discussed a few basic Christian beliefs; and even those I have not tried to argue for, because they are, I believe, most properly understood as mysteries. Part of the evidence for their truth is that they exceed our power to understand them fully and demonstrate their truth.

If, however, someone wishes to know why these mysteries should be accepted, an answer can be given. They are not grasped in a blind leap of faith. They are accepted because of the faith Christians place in Jesus. (See Chapters Seven and Eight.) Because we believe Jesus is the Son of God, we accept the Bible as a special, authoritative revelation of God. (See Chapter Nine.) These mysteries are believed because they are taught in the Bible, and there is no reason to believe them unless one accepts the Bible as a trustworthy revelation from God.

Many people react in a negative, almost visceral, manner to the word *authority*. To them, relying on authority means abandoning reason, almost a returning to superstition. It is true that authorities should not be accepted or chosen blindly. But relying on authority is hardly abandoning reason. Every one of us relies on authority for most all of what we believe. If an authority has been shown to be trustworthy, then it is highly reasonable to trust in the authority and unreasonable not to trust, especially when the authority knows far more than we do about a subject. Anyone who has trusted Jesus as Lord and Savior can hardly help but regard him as a trustworthy authority. Anyone who accepts *his* authority can hardly reject his view of the Old Testament or the writings of Jesus' followers, who were given special authority by Jesus to carry on his work. In the end authority sticks in our throat, not because it is unreasonable, but because we want to be our own final authority.

This is the good news and the bad news. The bad news is that I can become a Christian only by recognizing the limits of my

rational powers and humbly accepting and experiencing the truth
about God that he himself deems it important to reveal. The good
news is that I do not have to fully understand or rationally prove
God's mysteries to be a Christian. I merely have to be willing to
learn from him as a child learns from a trusted parent. I merely
have to understand enough to be able to worship him and serve
him as I ought.

CHAPTER THIRTEEN

Making a Commitment

There is a point at which everything becomes simple and there is no longer any question of choice, because all you have staked will be lost if you look back. Life's point of no return.

Dag Hammarskjöld, *Markings*

The Archbishop of Canterbury: Jesus is the Son of God, you know.
Jane Fonda: Maybe he is for you, but he's not for me.
Archbishop: Well, either he is or he isn't.

Conversation on the Dick Cavett Show

JIM SWUNG TO the left and stared straight ahead, avoiding any eye contact with the earnest young people who were buttonholing other departing passengers. "Why can't they keep these Hare Krishnas out of the airports?" he wondered. He supposed it had to do with civil rights in a public place, or some such thing.

The Hare Krishnas' presence bothered Jim for more than one reason. He was in a hurry to catch his flight back to school and didn't really want to be harangued, much less to purchase any of their literature. But the Krishnas were also a disturbing reminder of Jim's own religious indecision and impossible-to-ignore evidence of the plurality of options facing him.

He certainly was much more serious about religion than he had been at the beginning of his vacation. He had enjoyed several good talks with Holly about her newfound faith, and he had gained a real respect for her commitment. He was surprised to discover how much she had thought about her faith and how sensible some of her ideas sounded.

It now seemed plausible to him that Christianity might really be true. Maybe he had been too hasty in throwing out his faith. Still, something in him didn't feel ready to make a commitment. He wasn't sure just why, but one thing that still bothered him was the sheer multiplicity of religions. Surely if he had been born in India, the odds were that he would be a Hindu. (Though he had been surprised to find the Indian student in his dorm was a Christian!) It seemed somehow a little arbitrary for him to adopt Christianity. In any case, it didn't seem likely to him that one religion could contain the final truth. In fact, the whole idea that one religion could be true struck him as somewhat arrogant and intolerant. It seemed to him that it was exactly this kind of "dogmatic" belief that produced a lot of the strife in the world, in places like the Middle East and the former Yugoslavia, for example.

Is a Religion True if It Helps Me Live "Truly"?

The final intellectual barrier to a genuine Christian commitment on Jim's part is a daunting one indeed. Many issues are hidden in the indecision that his encounter with the Hare Krishnas pushed to the forefront of his consciousness.

First, there is the worry that regarding one religion as true is ethnocentric or provincial. Surely, one might think, it's not reasonable to think that God has revealed himself to one portion of the globe and ignored the rest. To view my own culture's religion as the final truth seems arrogant. It seems more reasonable to accept all religions as true in their own way.

What could it mean to say that "all religions are true"? I know of two distinct ways in which this might be understood.

One way is to say that all religions are true (or can be true) because none of them is true. That sounds paradoxical, but the underlying meaning is not. Some people have urged that it is a mistake to think of religions being true or false *in themselves*. In reality it is the lives of religious believers that can be said to be true or false. If a person's religion inspires that person to live truly and authentically, perhaps we should say that the religion is "true" for that person. In this sense every religion may be "true" in that each of them may provide the motivation for a meaningful, worthwhile life for at least some of its followers.

This line of thought contains several grave difficulties. First of all, there is the problem of deciding what it means to live "truly and authentically." An honest look at the world's religions shows that there are huge disagreements as to what such a life would be like. Some religions teach that to be blessed one must refrain from all worldly involvements, while others teach that one must be wholly absorbed in human problems. Some teach that one must refrain from sex, alcoholic beverages, and other things, while other religions actually make these part of their religious rites. To choose one of these views of how life is to be lived as the correct one would seem to be another way of making one religion the final truth. But if we do not have a clear, agreed-on sense of what it means to say that a religion inspires its adherents to live truly, then the claim that all religions can be true if only they inspire their followers to live truly turns out to have no clear meaning.

An even more fundamental objection to this line of thought is that is confuses truth with usefulness. Christians, for example, believe that Jesus was the Son of God and that he died and rose again to save us from sin and death. Now what might it mean to say that those claims aren't true in themselves but they "become true" if they inspire Christians to live "true lives"? To put it baldly, it means that these claims are false, but it is psychologically useful for Christians to believe them anyway. Even if it were true that believing these claims was psychologically useful, that would hardly give anyone who cared about truth a reason to believe in Christianity if the claims are false. In fact, as soon as I realized that these claims weren't true *in themselves* but only that it was useful for me to believe them, I would cease to believe them, and they would thereby cease to be useful. On this interpretation, to say that "all religions are true" in the end *is* to say that no religion is true. We cannot evade the question of truth by looking only at what seems useful.

Do All Religions Point to the Same Truth at Bottom?

The second way of interpreting the claim that all religions are true is to say that all religions at bottom teach the same truth. On the surface this looks unpromising, since the different religions seem to teach very different (and incompatible) things. However, this thesis can be made more plausible.

Perhaps God or the Divine or Ultimate Reality completely exceeds the grasp of the human mind. Maybe we can never know what God is like in himself. The different religions of the world seem to offer differing pictures of God, but maybe these are simply pictures of aspects of God, or the way God *appears* to a particular group of people. Perhaps they are like the famous apparently conflicting descriptions of an elephant produced by a group of blind people. (Some said it was like a wall, others said it was like a tree, others a thick rope, and so on.)

This way of thinking is appealing to many. It seems very modest, with its emphasis on the way God in himself exceeds the grasp of the human mind. In a way Christians agree with that. Since God is infinite it is unlikely that our finite minds can fully comprehend his nature (which is why so much of God's self-revelation is a mystery to us).

How are we to understand the transcendence of God? Is God *completely* unknowable? If so, how could we know that? It would seem that we would have to know at least *something* about God even to know that we can never know him completely. Or, for that matter, we need to know something about him even to know what (or whom) we are talking about when we say "*God* is too great to be fully understood by finite humans." Christians therefore do not agree that God is *completely* unknowable. We may not be able to comprehend him, but we are able to know him (and some things about him) with his help as he reveals himself to us.

To say that God is completely unknowable may seem modest, but actually it is a very immodest claim. The person who makes it is claiming that all of the religions in the world who claim to have some accurate knowledge of God are wrong, and to know *that* is to know quite a lot.

If God is not completely unknowable, then we must take seriously the claims of various religions to offer knowledge of him. Among these claims is the claim of Christianity that Jesus is the supreme route to knowing God, because he is God himself. It is an essential part of Christian faith that Jesus is God in a unique and exclusive way. It follows from this that all religions cannot be equally true. If all religions are equally true, then Christianity is false, and therefore not all religions are true.

For better or worse, Christianity makes claims that cannot be evaded. There is no way to avoid a decision. Either Jesus is who he says he is, in which case Christianity is true in a way no other religion is; or else Jesus is not who he says he is, in which case the very essence of Christianity is not true at all.

This does not mean that Christians say that all other religions are completely false. God may very well reveal himself in different ways to different people in different cultures. There is no reason to deny that other religions may embody some true awareness of God. But a follower of Jesus must regard Jesus himself as God's final, decisive revelation of himself.

Nor does this mean that Christians must be intolerant or arrogant, or that they are uninterested in dialogue with members of other religions. True tolerance and respect require an honest recognition of differences, and genuine dialogue begins with a frank admission of differences and a willingness to respect sincere disagreement. It would seem rather that it is the people who say "all religions say the same thing" who are intolerant, because they will not allow their partners in dialogue to disagree with them.

It is also a mistake to think of Christianity as a part of Western culture, or to imagine that to become a Christian is to endorse a kind of cultural chauvinism. Christianity began as a Middle Eastern religion. It has at all times had adherents from diverse cultures. It is true that many Westerners have often mixed up their Christianity and their culture, to the detriment of both. However, today the center of gravity of Christianity has already shifted from Europe and North America to Asia, Africa, and Latin America. The church is not only large in these areas; in the opinion of many it is more vibrant and healthy there than in the West.

Of course it is true that much of the sectarian violence in the world is mixed up with and often justified by religious belief. As I noted in Chapter Eleven, where I discussed slavery, sexism, and other social evils, sinful human beings have an inveterate tendency to try to justify or "baptize" their own actions by cloaking them in whatever ultimate values they hold. For most people those values are religious. Regrettably, many Christians, or at least people who think of themselves as Christians, have thought that their faith justified violence and intolerance towards others. However, it is hard to see how genuine followers of a crucified God, who saved by suffering injustice and forgave his enemies even while dying, can think that their faith justifies violent repression of others.

Making a Reasonable Choice?

Suppose that Jim realizes the necessity of a choice regarding his religious stance. Not all religions can be true, and it is quite possible that one is true in a unique way. How should he go about making a decision as to what he should believe?

To some degree at least, the decision is not really his to make. To a large extent, belief is not under our voluntary control. I cannot make myself believe things that I know (or think I know) to be false. For example, I could not make myself believe that Bill Clinton never existed, even if I were offered a great sum of money should I turn the trick. (I might pretend to have a belief I didn't have, but that would be quite different.) The fact that belief is usually not under our voluntary control fits quite well with the normal Christian experience that when people finally find God, they discover that it was really God who found them.

Still, though we can't usually directly control our beliefs, we can control them indirectly over time, by thinking about evidence we have, by looking for new evidence, and by acting on the beliefs we are acquiring (more on this later). And perhaps sometimes we can directly form a belief. There are times, I think, when I find myself on the verge of believing something, or in the process of forming a belief, and yet the belief does not yet *feel* like a belief. I'm not yet really committed, and yet I sense within me the power to make a commitment, to give what is only a belief-in-the-making firmness and solidity. It is this experience, I think, that converts to Christianity are often describing when they speak of a decision to believe in Christ.

But when is such a decision a reasonable one? When is it reasonable for people like Jim and Holly to make a decision for Christ? This question could, of course, lead to a lengthy philosophical discussion indeed. Still, I think the answer is clear enough to a person who considers the issue with common sense, though the implications of the answer are different for different people. Specifically the situation of the person who is already committed to Christianity (or some other faith) is different from that of a person who is still searching for something to believe in.

The general answer is that a commitment to a position is reasonable for a person when that position makes more sense than any of its rivals, judged by all the evidence that is reasonably available to that person. We have in this book traced out the major kinds of evidence that bear on Christianity. We have looked at the experiences of the contingency and purposiveness of nature, at the experience of the moral "ought," and at the qualities and desires in human nature that are clues to the reality of God. We have looked at the objective evidence for Jesus being the Son of God, and the subjective evidence that lies buried in the needs and desires of our hearts. We have seen that a strong case can be made for the reasonableness of Christian faith.

We have also looked at the supposedly negative evidence, the arguments against Christianity from science and evil. Here we have seen that science, far from undermining Christian faith, deepens our awareness of the intricate design in nature that points to God. Evil and suffering, while often baffling and troublesome, are not decisive evidence against the truth of Christianity for those who have reason to believe in a good God who loved us enough to share in our human sufferings.

The overall case is clear, therefore, for someone who honestly looks at all the evidence and is genuinely concerned for the truth. Belief in God is coherent with all we know about ourselves and our universe. It contradicts no known facts, and it makes sense of many things that would otherwise be inexplicable. If God exists, we might very well expect him to reveal himself to us in some clearer way, and Christianity claims that he has done just that. The focus of that revelation is Jesus Christ, and we have seen that the story of the life, death, and resurrection of Jesus as told in the Bible presents us with a strong claim that forces us to decide whether he was truly the Son of God, or else a madman or a charlatan. To a person who senses her own need for God, who understands that she would be unable to please and know God if left to her own devices, a commitment to Jesus as Savior seems eminently reasonable.

To the person who is already committed to Christ, this means that the commitment is a reasonable one. To such a person, I would say, "Stop worrying about the fact that you may have believed initially because of family or peer pressure, or simply because you knew no alternative." The reasonableness of a belief is not determined by its origins, but by a willingness to honestly and thoughtfully reflect on that belief. If you have read this far in a book such as this, you are clearly the sort of person who is interested in doing just that. Keep on with your commitment and show that the commitment is a reasonable one by continuing to honestly look at objections and problems as they arise.

In a similar way, I would say to the Jims who may be reading this book, "Take a new look at the case for Christianity, and if you can, commit yourself. Recognize that your indecision may not be grounded in a lack of evidence, but in our natural human pride, which rebels against God and his authority and continually seeks to hide its rebelliousness from itself."

Both those who are committed and those who are considering committing themselves should avoid at all costs one fatal trap. I call it the "If-I-were-someone-else syndrome." It is so tempting to reason that if I were someone else, brought up in a different family, or a different country, then things would look different. While it is true that I would have different beliefs if I were someone else, this line of thought leads only to a paralyzing skepticism. *You are not anyone else.* You are yourself. It is your life that is on the line. You must decide what seems true to you on the basis of the experiences and evidence available to you.

The If-I-were-someone-else syndrome is at bottom a futile attempt to escape our human finitude. All of us are finite individuals who have had a unique history. It is not possible for us to have had the experiences of everyone or to have read all the books dealing with any subject. If Christianity is true, then there is a God who holds people responsible for their actions. If there are people who because of the circumstances of their lives are prevented from knowing God, we may be confident that God will treat such people lovingly and justly. What is crucial to remember is that God will hold you responsible for the evidence and opportunities that were available to you as an individual. It is not your responsibility to decide for those in radically different circumstances.

Faith and Doubt

But what if I have doubts? Many people, whether Christians or those considering a commitment to Christianity, are confused about the relation of faith and doubt. They think that if they have doubts, then their faith is not genuine, or even that they shouldn't commit themselves.

To understand doubt, we must begin with faith. We have spoken a great deal in this book about believing in the truth of Christianity. This is quite proper because there are many things that Christians do believe: that God is real, and Jesus is God's Son, for example. However, speaking about the truth of Christianity in this way can be misleading, because it may convey the idea that Christian faith is something purely intellectual: that it consists solely in believing some propositions to be true. The truth is that a Christian does believe certain propositions to be true; such beliefs are a necessary expression of faith. However, someone who only has intellectual beliefs is not a true Christian.

A true Christian is someone who comes to believe certain things in the process of coming to believe *in* Jesus. She believes certain things because she has committed herself to him and decided to *live* as his follower because of her trust in him and love for him. It is this commitment that is properly described as Christian faith.

True faith then is a trust that must express itself in such things as actions, emotions, and attitudes as well as beliefs. This does not mean, of course, that you must follow Christ perfectly to be a Christian. It means that if you are a genuine believer in Christ, you will be different in some ways than you otherwise would have been.

This fact that faith must express itself in action implies several important things. One is that faith can be decisive and total, even if a person does not have totally decisive evidence for his beliefs. This is because actions have an all-or-nothing character. Either they are done or they are not done.

An example or two might help. Suppose I am having some difficulties — say, severe depression. I need help, and I talk to my friends about several alternative therapists. I consider the evidence for the effectiveness of Freudian therapy, client-centered therapy, and behavioral therapy. It seems to me that one brand of therapy has the best credentials, and I am inclined to trust one therapist more than the others, but the case is not black and white. There is something to be said for the others. What should I do?

If I am going to seek help, it seems to me I ought to go to the therapist who offers the most promise of help, in light of all the evidence I have. One thing I should *not* do is hedge my bets here. I ought not secretly to see a second therapist while working with the first. Nor should I enter the therapy program prepared to terminate at the first sign of trouble. The fact is, if I want help at all, I must commit myself and be prepared to stick with my commitment for at least a reasonable period. Only in this way can I give the therapist a fair trial and good test. And only in this way can I reasonably expect to get help.

The analogy of marriage is perhaps even more apt for religious faith. Imagine a young woman is trying to decide whether to marry a young man. Certainly she considers whether it seems reasonable to think that this man will be a good friend and faithful partner. She will never have absolute proof. But if she decides to marry at all, it would be unreasonable for her to withhold her full commitment to the marriage on the grounds that she has no proof it will work out. The fact is she must either marry or not marry, and marriage should be an all-or-nothing affair. Regardless of whether her evidence is weak or powerful, if she commits herself, it should be a wholehearted commitment. And notice that once again, as in the case of the therapist, the wholehearted commitment is essential if she is to give her belief in the man a fair test.

Of course I don't mean that such a wholehearted commitment blinds a person to negative evidence. A woman committed to marriage should not deceive herself about a man who abuses her. But an honest openness to evidence is compatible with a determination to make the relationship work.

Two lessons are to be drawn from these two examples. One is that wholehearted commitment can be reasonable even when some doubts exist about the finality of the logical evidence. The second is that a wholehearted commitment may provide a means for resolving those doubts.

Christians who have doubts about their faith should not necessarily see this as a sign that their faith is weak. Such doubts may simply be an expression of the human finitude we sometimes try to escape in the if-I-were-someone-else syndrome. The test as to whether we have genuine faith in Christ is not whether we ever have an intellectual doubt. The real test is whether we are willing to obey Christ, to act as his follower, in spite of our doubts. Doubt, depending on its causes and how it is dealt with, can even be healthy at times.

This should, I think, be encouraging to Jim. When he is asked to make a commitment to Christ, he is not being asked to deny any intellectual problems he may have, nor is he being asked to promise that he will never have such doubts in the future. He should know that he will be encouraged to consider and resolve his intellectual difficulties honestly.

Jim may also get some insight from this as to how it may be

possible for him to resolve his indecision and make a commitment. Our actions stem from our beliefs, but they also help us to form our beliefs. We commit ourselves by beginning to act as a committed person would act. If Jim can do this, he may find many of his intellectual problems look very different.

Christianity has always maintained that the truth about God cannot be discovered merely through detached contemplation, but is learned through doing. As Jesus said to his disciples, "If you hold to my teaching, you are really my disciples. Then you will know the truth, and the truth will set you free" (John 8:31-32). In the context it becomes clear that when Jesus speaks of "holding" to his teaching, he means *living* in accordance with his commands.

This is hardly surprising. We noted already (in Chapters One and Three) that it is unlikely that God would impose a knowledge of himself on those who do not wish to love and serve him. It is reasonable then that a deeper knowledge of God will be offered to those who respond positively to the insights God has already offered them.

Acting on a commitment then serves the twofold purpose of resolving doubts and making possible an honest testing of the commitment. It does the former partly because our actions do shape our beliefs. Psychologists have verified that this is correct. Marxists and other radical political groups understand this clearly. That is why new recruits are generally assigned some very public actions, such as selling literature on the street. The visible public actions solidify the recruits' convictions and resolve doubts.

The lesson is that if you think a good case can be made for Christianity and want to be a Christian, but somehow just can't believe, you should simply start to act like a Christian. This doesn't mean that you will immediately be able to exhibit the difficult, radical, self-denying love God wishes to infuse into his children. It means rather that you should begin to pray. Meet with other Christians. Participate in public worship. Study the Bible. Try to follow its teachings as best you can. You may soon find yourself believing.

But a commitment to Christ does more than merely firm up belief for psychological reasons. It provides a genuine test of the claims of Christianity to be true. Christianity promises that a commitment to Jesus will provide you with new insight into your self, an understanding of your own deepest needs and desires. It does not promise worldly success or freedom from distress or anxiety. It does promise an assurance that your guilt has been forgiven (but not that you will never feel guilty), that you are accepted by God, and that you have the resources to experience more and more of that eternal life with God, now and after death, that you want so deeply. (Though you may have to sweep aside those superficial cravings that threaten to crowd it out to discover that this is what you want.) It offers you a chance to know God and yourself.

If Christianity cannot provide these things, it is false. Commitment to it holds out the promise of a meaningful test and evidence of a type that the uncommitted person can never hope to possess. But the rewards of such a commitment cannot be spelled out simply in the language of reasoning and argument; it is not simply a matter of gaining evidence but of *knowing God*.

What is it you want out of life? Will money satisfy you? Fame and honor? Do you live for erotic love? Why not search your heart to find out if the divine suitor is what you ultimately want? Of course, Jesus is also the one whom you *don't* want to find, the one who promises to turn your life upside down by freeing you from the need to play god. So expect to find resistance as you try to commit yourself to him. Remember the deep truth of Jesus' words: the same truth exemplified in his life and death. Life comes through dying. He who would find his life must be prepared to lose it, and he who loses his life in God will find it. Dying is never easy, but it is the path to eternal life with God.

Suggestions for Further Reading

Other general treatments of the reasonableness of Christian faith:

Lewis, C. S. *Mere Christianity*. New York: Macmillan, 1952; London: Collins, 1955.

Moreland, J. P. *Scaling the Secular City: A Defense of Christianity*. Grand Rapids: Baker Book House, 1987.

Purtill, Richard. *Reason to Believe*. Grand Rapids: Eerdmans, 1974.

Sire, James. *Why Should Anyone Believe Anything at All?* Downers Grove, IL: InterVarsity Press, 1994.

Introductory treatments of the philosophical issues that bear on the reasonableness of Christian faith:

Evans, C. Stephen. *Philosophy of Religion: Thinking about Faith*. Downers Grove, IL: InterVarsity Press; Leicester, Eng.: InterVarsity Press, 1985.

Mavrodes, George. *Belief in God: A Study in the Epistemology of Religion*. Rev. ed. New York: University Press of America, 1983.

Purtill, Richard. *Thinking about Religion*. Englewood Cliffs, NJ: Prentice-Hall, 1978.

On the general problem of knowledge and when belief is reasonable:

Wolfe, David. *Epistemology: The Justification of Belief.* Downers Grove, IL: InterVarsity Press; Leicester, Eng.: Inter-Varsity Press, 1982.

Wolterstorff, Nicholas. *Reason within the Bounds of Religion.* 2nd ed. Grand Rapids: Eerdmans, 1984.

On the contingency and purposiveness of nature as clues to God's reality:

Casserly, J. V. L. *Graceful Reason.* Greenwich, CT: Seabury Press, 1954.

Farrer, Austin. *A Science of God?* London: Geoffrey Bles, 1966.

Taylor, Richard. "God," in *Metaphysics* (ch. 10). 3rd ed. Englewood Cliffs, NJ: Prentice-Hall, 1983.

Also see Evans, *Philosophy of Religion* (chs. 2, 3); and Purtill, *Thinking about Religion* (ch. 3).

On human nature and human desires as clues to God's reality:

Berger, Peter L. *A Rumor of Angels.* Garden City, NY: Doubleday, 1970.

Evans, C. Stephen. *Existentialism: The Philosophy of Despair and the Quest for Hope.* Dallas, TX: Probe Books, 1984. (Revised edition of *Despair: A Moment or a Way of Life?* Downers Grove, IL: InterVarsity Press, 1971.)

Kreeft, Peter. *Heaven: The Heart's Deepest Longing.* San Francisco: Harper and Row, 1980.

Lewis, C. S. *Miracles.* New York: Macmillan; London: Collins/Fontana, 1960.

Lewis, C. S. "The Weight of Glory," in *The Weight of Glory and Other Addresses.* New York: Macmillan, 1980; also in *Screwtape Proposes a Toast and Other Pieces.* London: Collins/Fontana, 1965.

On the question of Jesus: Is he really God?

Green, Michael, ed. *The Truth of God Incarnate.* London: Hodder
and Stoughton, 1977.

Kreeft, Peter. *Between Heaven and Hell.* Downers Grove, IL: Inter-
Varsity Press, 1982.

Stott, John. *The Authentic Jesus.* Downers Grove, IL: InterVarsity
Press, 1986.

Stott, John. *Basic Christianity.* 2nd ed. Downers Grove, IL: Inter-
Varsity Press; Leicester, Eng.: Inter-Varsity Press, 1975.

Bruce, F. F. *Jesus: Lord and Savior.* Downers Grove, IL: Inter-
Varsity Press; London: Hodder and Stoughton, 1986.

On the reliability and authority of the Bible:

Blomberg, Craig. *The Historical Reliability of the Gospels.*
Downers Grove, IL: InterVarsity Press, 1987.

Bruce, F. F. *The New Testament Documents: Are They Reliable?*
Rev. ed. Downers Grove, IL: InterVarsity Press; Leicester,
Eng.: Inter-Varsity Press, 1960.

Carnell, Edward John. *The Case for Orthodox Theology* (chs. 1-3,
7). Philadelphia: Westminster, 1959.

Lewis, C. S. "Modern Theology and Biblical Criticism," in *Christian Reflections.* Grand Rapids: Eerdmans; London: Geoffrey
Bles, 1967.

Marshall, I. Howard. *I Believe in the Historical Jesus.* Grand
Rapids: Eerdmans, 1977.

On miracles and the supernatural:

Swinburne, Richard. *The Concept of Miracle.* London: Macmillan,
1970.

Also see C. S. Lewis, *Miracles;* Evans, *Philosophy of Religion* (ch.
5); and Purtill, *Thinking about Religion* (ch. 5).

On the problem of evil:

Lewis, C. S. *The Problem of Pain*. New York: Macmillan, 1962; London: Geoffrey Bless, 1940.

Peterson, Michael. *Evil and the Christian God*. Grand Rapids: Baker, 1982.

Yancey, Philip. *Where Is God when It Hurts?* Grand Rapids: Zondervan, 1977.

Also see George Mavrodes, "The Problem of Evil," in *Belief in God*.

On the charge that Christianity is unscientific:

Fischer, Robert. *God Did It But How? Relationships between the Bible and Science*. La Mirada, CA: Cal Media, 1981.

Hummel, Charles. *The Galileo Connection*. Downers Grove, IL: InterVarsity Press, 1986.

MacKay, Donald M. *The Clockwork Image*. Downers Grove, IL: InterVarsity Press; Leicester, Eng.: Inter-Varsity Press, 1974.

Ratzsch, Del. *Philosophy of Science: The Natural Sciences in Christian Perspective*. Downers Grove, IL: InterVarsity Press; Leicester, Eng.: Inter-Varsity Press, 1986.

On the charge that Christianity is a form of wish fulfillment:

Farmer, Herbert H. "The Psychological Theory of Religion," in *Towards Belief in God* (ch. 10). New York: Macmillan, 1978.

Rowe, William L. "Freud and Religious Belief," in *Philosophy of Religion: An Introduction*. Belmont, CA: Wadsworth, 1978.

Also see C. S. Lewis, "The Weight of Glory"; Evans, *The Philosophy of Religion* (ch. 6); and Purtill, *Reason to Believe* (ch. 2).

On the charge that Christianity is a reactionary social or political tool:

Farmer, H. H. "The Sociological Theory of Religion," in *Towards Belief in God* (ch. 9).
Also see Evans, *Philosophy of Religion* (ch. 6).

On the central Christian doctrines:

Lewis, C. S. *What Christians Believe.* Book two of *Mere Christianity.*
Milne, Bruce. *Know the Truth: A Handbook of Christian Belief.* Downers Grove, IL: InterVarsity Press; Leicester, Eng.: Inter-Varsity Press, 1982.

On faith, doubt, and commitment in a pluralistic world:

Anderson, Norman. *Christianity and World Religions.* Downers Grove, IL: InterVarsity Press; Leicester, Eng.: Inter-Varsity Press, 1984.
Guinness, Os. *In Two Minds.* Downers Grove, IL: InterVarsity Press, 1976. Published also as *Doubt.* Berkhamsted, Eng.: Lion, 1976.
Newbigin, Lesslie. *The Finality of Christ.* Richmond, VA: John Knox, 1969.
Also see Evans, *Philosophy of Religion* (ch. 8).